A new physical and mental health!

What is the vegetarian way of life? Not merely a form of diet, it is a practical and rewarding life style that influences every aspect of living—friendship, love, choice of profession, personal interests. It is a possible way to better health, more energy, and an even-tempered approach to life's problems.

Hans Holzer offers new insights into the emotional aspects of eating, correcting ill-health naturally, the role of health foods in diet, the importance of periodic purification, combatting "low ebb" periods, and increasing sexual endurance.

Try it! It *can* work to make all of life better, richer, healthier, happier—and maybe even *longer!*

Professor Hans Holzer, who teaches at the New York Institute of Technology, is the author of 33 books, including *Star in the East, Window to the Past, Charismatics,* and *The Aquarian Age.* An archaeologist and historian by training, he is a lecturer on various topics through the S. Hurok Speakers Group, and a frequent guest on television and radio talk shows.

THE VEGETARIAN WAY OF LIFE

How the Proper Foods Determine Your Outlook, Health, and Fulfillment

Hans Holzer

 PYRAMID BOOKS • NEW YORK

THE VEGETARIAN WAY OF LIFE

A PYRAMID BOOK

Second printing July, 1974

ISBN: 0-515-03234-4

Pyramid Books are published by Pyramid Communications, Inc. Its trademarks, consisting of the word "Pyramid" and the portrayal of a pyramid, are registered in the United States Patent Office.

Printed in the United States of America

PYRAMID COMMUNICATIONS, INC.
919 Third Avenue
New York, New York 10022, U.S.A.

Table of Contents

INTRODUCTION

As I look through the literature on the vegetarian approach to eating and cooking, I find that other authors in this field invariably assume that a vegetarian knows why he or she is a vegetarian and that it is none of his business to tell them anything about his motivation or the implications of being a vegetarian. These authors proceed immediately to the subject at hand, which is fine, if you're very hungry. The subject, of course, is what to do when you *are* a vegetarian. What sort of foods should be eaten, how they should be prepared, what to do and what not to do in connection wth one's vegetarian approach to eating. Many authors connect being a vegetarian with being interested in health foods, which is understandable, since the two frequently go together. But not always; there are two distinct approaches to nutrition. About this, anon.

So the first reason for writing this book was to fill a void with a basic book on vegetarian philosophy, and on the implications being vegetarian has in other departments of life. The second reason for committing to paper my thoughts on vegetarianism, most of them going back over many years and ripened under the influence of reality, of propaganda from all sides, and by that internal maturing process that inevitably comes with getting a little older, was that I felt, without undue modesty, that I ought to share my thoughts and experiences with the broader public. This became especially advisable when I realized that I had a considerable following among people interested in extrasensory perception and allied subjects. Having "led" them thus far into the realms of the formerly supernatural, and demonstrated to them that psychic phenomena are perfectly natural and part of human experience, I felt tempted to take them a step further into the esoteric aspects of physical life, the areas of our ordinary lives which so many do not fully understand or enjoy simply because they haven't given them enough thought. It occurred to me that people interested in various phases of the occult would inevitably come to a point where they would question, along with other fallacies of the past, the conventional environment of their upbringing, including a standard diet, partaking of meat and other fleshly products, and never giving the vegetarian approach a second thought.

For those who wish to complete their liberation from orthodox life by adding a nutritional aspect to their acquired wisdom, and to those who are not even ESP fans or students of the occult but nevertheless have questions about their own diet, a book such as this may be welcome indeed; it will give them, perhaps, the reasons for what they may have felt vaguely for sometime past, or for what they now feel, and in giving them a solid basis for their unexpressed attitudes towards ordinary diets, help them come to terms with what to the majority of people is still an unusual way of life. Eventually, of course, that majority will shrink and it is my fervent hope that in the years to come larger sections of the population will realize that the way to good health on all levels lies indeed in the Vegetarian Way of Life.

CHAPTER ONE
WHY DOES MAN HAVE TO EAT?

If man were an entirely spiritual being, existing on a mental plane, the need for gross food would clearly be absent. As a matter of fact, if we are to believe those who have communicated with us from beyond the grave—and many have under conditions making these communications seemingly authentic—then there is no need among spiritual beings for physical food.

The reason why is this: when man dies he leaves behind him his physical body, but assumes a finer, thinner body called the etheric body. This inner body, contained all his life on earth in the physical body, contains also the personality, the soul if you wish, and goes immediately to the next phase of existence. In that phase thoughts have three-dimensional reality. Everything a man is able to project in thought is real not only to himself but to others in his world. Only when it is viewed from the gross physical world in which we live while in the physical body does it appear to be two-dimensional or shadowy. That is because we are not able to partake of the non-physical world in the same way those who are in it are able to view it. After thirty years of intensive study of psychic phenomena, I am firmly convinced of the reality of this other half of our world, frequently referred to as the non-physical world.

If the etheric body is an exact duplicate of the physical body, containing all the organs and peculiarities of the physical body, then one would expect it to contain similar needs for the intake of

food and of course for the elimination of same.
Quite obviously, there would be no need for a stomach or an intestinal tract if no food were taken into
the etheric body. Yet, from all the testimony
known to me, at least the discarnates, or communi-
cating spirits, described their food problems in similar terms: if they feel like eating and drinking, they
can do so, of course, but the need to do so no longer
exists. It would appear, then, that the duplicate organs in the etheric body are there to accommodate
the individual immediately after passing from the
physical into the next stage. For some time afterwards, the habit pattern of food and drink intake
remains with most individuals who have passed
over; they partake of foods and drink that duplicate those they are familiar with on earth. The
foods "over there" are finer and better and definitely healthier than the ones we have in our world.
The liquids available to them are also of a better
kind but they are still food and drink. At a certain
point in their ongoing development, discarnate individuals no longer think of food and drink as a
daily occurrence. At that point the intake of food or
drink becomes a pleasurable one, no longer dictated
by bodily needs.

This seems to be the point: so long as food and
drink are necessities to maintain life, they remain
more or less tied to a routine, and thus a kind of a
drudgery. When the need for their intake is absent,
they develop into a pleasurable experience, optional
as to time, conditions and amount. In this respect
the food and drink situation beyond the physical
world seems similar to the need for sleep.

From the testimonial material available to me, it
appears that day and night do not follow each other
the way they do on earth. The world into which we

all must go after dissolution of the physical body is forever lit by a superior source of light. Under the circumstances darkness is absent, except, of course, in those areas where it represents lack of enlightenment—darkness of the soul, so to speak, and other negative psychological states. We must remember that the world into which we go after physical death is a thought world in which mental states and conditions are represented directly to our sensory organs. The brighter our own development is, the brighter the world around us will appear. The darker our thoughts are, the darker it will be.

Those who wish to continue their pattern of wakefulness and sleep can do so, of course. For them, beds are forever ready in their houses, all of them built by thoughts. They may rest in the sleep state or do without it if they're ready to do so. As a matter of fact, at the beginning, when individuals pass over to the next stage, especially when they did not expect to find such a stage, they are put to sleep for a short time to give them additional rest in preparation for their further enlightenment. But in the long run, purely physical conditions, such as food, drink and sleep fade away and are replaced by a continuum of awareness in which values different from earth conditions predominate.

But so long as we are in the physical body, no matter how esoteric we feel about the universe, no matter how highly developed our individual consciousness already is, the basic needs of the body must be met. The physical body is so constructed that it needs nourishment to maintain its functions. The foods we eat, and the liquids we drink, are broken down in the body, by *resident chemicals*, in order to make them available to the various departments of our body. The system is absolutely ingenious and perfect. When it doesn't work, don't blame nature, blame yourself and the inadequacies you permit to exist in you and in the sources of your foodstuffs.

By taking the valuable substances out of the foodstuffs and the liquids we take in we make them available as an energy supply to the bodily organs and their functions, leaving the residue of the foodstuffs and liquids to be removed through the alimentary and intestinal canals. Naturally, a proper balance between intake and outgo is essential to the functioning of the body. Although this is not the place to dwell upon it, a majority of diseases are due not so much to the invasion of foreign bacteria or viruses but to the presence of unnecessary and dangerous toxins the the bodily system, poisons which haven't been removed as they should be and begin to destroy the host's body.

Of course, if we could obtain the raw materials taken from the foodstuffs and liquids by the chemicals in our bodies and partake of them directly, without the need for the chemicals to extract them from foodstuffs and liquids, we would save those chemicals a lot of effort; unfortunately, this is impossible because synthetic building blocks, even if chemically identical with the real thing, lack the etheric counterparts and remain incomplete and thus worthless in terms of feeding the body. Synthesizing foodstuffs or the essences of foodstuffs is an erroneous practice that follows materialistic lines: in the belief that the physical body is all there is to man, disregarding the etheric body and soul within completely, some materialistically oriented scientists would also disregard the etheric qualities of foodstuffs taken in by man.

For it is a fact to remember, that every morsel of food, every liquid we drink has two sides to it: the material and the etheric side. Man is not the only living being endowed with an etheric counterpart, a second body within; animals, plants, in fact, everything in nature has an inner counterpart which continues to exist after the physical outer shell has been destroyed. When we partake of food we not only assimilate the material essences of that food in our bodies, but nourish our etheric bodies with the etheric essences of those same foods. When synthetic essences are offered the body, the etheric body is left to starve. The results are ill health, and lack of nourishment.

When we take food or drink into our system there are several processes taking place simultaneously within us. The most important is, of course, the immediate utilization of the essences in the foodstuffs and liquids so that they may be brought to the places where they are needed, the various organs and systems of the boly which run it. But there is another aspect to the intake of food and drink: as we view these foodstuffs and liquids, we receive certain visual impressions which in turn trigger certain mental images in our minds.

Every piece of food, every liquid represents an idea as well as a chemical compound. For instance it makes a difference whether a dish is beautifully prepared, well done, presented on an attractive plate in a most appetizing manner, or whether the same basic raw materials are eaten out of a brown paper bag. It makes a difference whether we are able to think of the salad we are about to eat as green and fresh or as shredded and packed in paper. In other words, the thoughts and opinions we have concerning the foods we eat, especially at the time when we eat them, play a role in how these foods will be utilized by the bodily system.

This is not to say we should pat the glutton on the shoulder and say, it is nice that you enjoy food so much; but it is true that a balanced enjoyment of the foods we eat is important for their proper assimilation. People who eat with disdain, simply because they must fill a void in themselves or because they realize that without food they will collapse, make very poor eaters. People who do their eating while doing something else, in order to save time, people who rush through their meals inordinately, as if they feel a meal is something that interferes with their other interests, are doing their bodies a disservice. This does not mean that a person who lingers over his food, and eats very slowly, is doing such a good job either; the food gets cold, the imagery drags because it takes too long from the moment the food is visualized through the sensory apparatus until it enters the body itself. The answer, then, lies in a balanced approach to eating: neither too fast nor too slow.

From the beginning of time, man had available to him various kinds of foods. The need to eat and drink is inborn in man; he requires no teaching to know that he has those needs. Stone Age man, however, satisfied those needs on the lowest possible level. He did not yet know how to cultivate anything, but he did know where foodstuffs could be found in nature. Consequently, he was a hunter and fisher. He realized that the flesh of animals and of fish would supply his body with its fuel. He also learned that certain plants could be eaten while others could not be. He came to these conclusions by trial and error as time went on. Undoubtedly, the most primitive of all men ate his food raw as he found it. Only later on did he realize that cooking his food would improve it, both as to taste and as to utilization. With the discovery of fire in the second stage of man's development came the ability to cook his food before eating.

If Darwin is right and man is but a further developed ape, somehow making the vital leap from the animal kingdom to the human kingdom, then man should have inherited the ape's food habits, but he did not; apes are not hunters nor fishermen. In fact, some of the largest beasts in nature are vegetarian, such as the elephant. If, on the other hand, man is a separate creation similar in physical appearance to the ape but a species unto himself, as I believe, then it is quite proper for him to develop his own eating habits. It would appear that man was belligerent and aggressive from the very beginning, subduing animals smaller than himself for the sole purpose of eating them. Early cave drawings point in that direction; early man was a hunter and fisherman.

Or was he? The assumption that the early cave drawings represent the dawn of man's development has been generally accepted; but at the same time we speak of the legend of Paradise, of Adam and Eve, the symbolic first couple, who lived a peaceful existence without killing animals for food. They lived on the fruits of their Garden of Eden. The memory of such a state of bliss runs through nearly all religions and philosophies. And as with most legendary concepts, there may be a good deal of truth behind it. We haven't discovered any cave drawings showing man in Paradise, eating fruit and nuts, simply because there weren't any caves in Paradise. If man lived in the Mediterranean "cradle of civilization" which some anthropologists and archaeologists assign to him, he had no need to eke out a difficult existence in caves; his world was full of the necessities of life. If this stage in man's development is accepted, then the Stone Age-cave concept of primitive man must come at a later time in man's development. Recent investigations have uncovered a surviving Stone Age tribe (the Tasaday tribe) that is totally vegetarian. Whether natural catastrophes forced man from his Mediterranean world into more austere surroundings or whether a separate strain of humanity developed independently in other climes, is debatable. I merely propose to my readers to consider the possibility that the Garden of Eden was by no means a fantasy, but a very real civilization predating the Stone Age.

Man has available to him two groups of foodstuffs. One, the largest in terms of variety, is the group of natural foodstuffs as found in nature. The second, dating back only a few hundred years, and coming into its own only nowadays, is the group of synthetic foodstuffs. Natural foodstuffs fall into three large subdivisions, animal-derived foodstuffs necessitating the killing of animals, plant-derived foodstuffs, necessitating the destruction of plants which, however, will grow again from the same roots or seeds, and finally animal and plant product foodstuffs, which are derived from either animals or plants without destroying the specific animal or plant.

The intake of animal-derived foodstuffs, meat, fish and products associated with them could be further divided into the meat of wild animals through the hunt and the meat of animals bred for slaughter. Synthetic foodstuffs are an attempt to imitate nature by putting together the essences of natural foodstuffs, reconstituted from separate chemical elements. Chemically, synthetic foodstuffs are identical with those found in nature. What is lacking, as I have already pointed out, is the etheric counterpart which comes only when the foodstuff is naturally grown. What is lacking, furthermore, is the knowledge of the way in which these separate substances are being mixed together. We do not exactly know this, for nature presents us with a *fait accompli*. The question of timing, speed, of circumstances under which these various elements are brought together seems to be very important to their efficiency after they have been blended. In the synthetic process none of these factors are taken into account, so long as the chemical formula reads the same.

This does not mean that a man-made food product cannot also be effective and healthful. Already there are on the market certain soybean products which are essentially synthetic foodstuffs, but they are put together with a deep and detailed knowledge of the interaction between various elements in foodstuffs and thus take into account factors other than mere chemical balance. Moreover, a synthetic food product derived from natural sources, such as these soy products are, is a different story from the synthetic products derived from purely chemical sources, starting from the basic elements rather than from existing natural foodstuffs. If there is any future in man-made food products, it lies almost exclusively with the foods derived from existing foodstuffs, but refined or arranged in various combinations to make them more palatable, or more useful, or more accessible.

Also, if such a product of the future is to succeed nutritionally, then the time element has to be taken into account, that is to say, whether the foodstuffs brought together in that particular combination will not deteriorate when packaged and left on the shelf for a period of time. Certain foodstuffs will, while others will not. The problem with preservatives of any kind is that they may preserve the foodstuffs, and prevent them from spoiling, but without protecting against the deterioration of nutritional values, let alone the etheric values invisible to the naked eye, or even to the instruments available to the chemist today. Under those circumstances I view the question of artificial foodstuffs with a great deal of caution.

There has always been a connection between food and religion. Whether the deity was the Great Mother Goddess of Stone Age man, supplemented by deities representing the forces of nature, or whether it was the Great God of the monotheistic religions, the Judeo-Christian concept or the Buddhist or Islamic concept of religion, the deity was implored to supply adequate foodstuffs for the people; the deity would bless the crop or the hunt and make it successful; and the deity must be offered a small portion of the blessings of the earth to keep it happy and content. In antiquity food offered the deity was either burned during a religious service, or, as with the more sophisticated religions such as Egypt's and Phoenicia's, absorbed into the bodies of the priests, thus sacrificed to the gods by osmosis—rather a roundabout way of satisfying the deity, but it kept the priests well fed. Religion also regulated fasts or the prohibition of certain foods because of religious concepts. In the Near East, pork was on the forbidden list not because it offended a particular god, but because the priests knew very well that it was unhealthy for the people. Had they simply suggested that pork was not a good idea on nutritional grounds, nobody would have listened to them. But to put the prohibition in the mouth of the god or couch it in the language of religious law made its acceptance imperative. Certain foodstuffs do not mix well in the body on purely chemical grounds, such as milk products and acids. Again, religious prohibition forbids the Hebrews and other Semitic people to eat both types of food at the same table. The majority of the people concerned do not even realize that there is a sound nutritional basis behind this prohibition. They accept the religious aspect and don't question it.

The offering of food and drink, both water and wine, is part of nearly all rituals in religious services. In many religions the food represents the body of the deity and the wine the blood of the supreme being; the latter idea has often been misconstrued to denote blood sacrifices or the like. Nothing could be further from the truth; the wine used in religious services need not even be red but can also be white. Partaking of a cake or cracker is by no means the invention of the Christian church. Many Pagan religions have a similar symbolic service, in which a piece of bread or a cracker is eaten by the communicants as part of their identification with the deity followed by a cup of wine which represents the lifeblood of man but at the same time the lifeblood of the deity.

All of these actions are purely symbolical. Blessing the food prior to partaking it goes back to the beginnings of mankind. In calling down the goodwill of the deity the food becomes an instrument of that deity. To this day, Christians and Hindus and Pagans and probably many other, less well-known faiths bring their food to the temple or church to be blessed. Whether that food is different because of the blessing is a debatable question. If the blessing is undertaken in the presence of a large congregation, then the thought energies of those desiring a favorable treatment for the food proffered may indeed change the molecular structure of the foodstuff in some fashion, just as the holy water in a church frequented by large numbers of people does show structural changes. On an individual level, drawing down divine blessing on the food one is to partake of may also have some effect on the foodstuff, but as yet we do not have the instrument to prove this; and yet, since energies and thought forms are involved, would it not seem natural that something does happen to the molecular structure of the food even if only one person prays for it?

Breaking bread with the congregation is a symbolic act of communion, in which the food represents the link between priest and community. By eating the food or sharing the wine, a part of the deity enters the communicants. Since the food or wine comes from the hands of the priest, the act of breaking bread or sharing the wine with the community also establishes a link between priest and community. The implication here is that, as the food nourishes the body, so the spiritual message and the enlightenment coming from the deity through the instrument of the priest will nourish the spirit of those participating in the service.

In the material world, food represents power. During the Roman republic, *aediles* or officials in charge of the wheat supply to metropolitan Rome were among the most powerful and politically corrupt individuals in the state. Roman emperors gained the favors of the masses by regular free food distributions, called *liberalities*. So proud were individual rulers of Rome of their distribution of food, that they even marked their coins with the number of liberalities they had distributed to the people over the years. Temples were erected to the Goddess of Liberality, symbolic of adequate food supplies.

Whereas the actual availability of foodstuffs represented individual power during the late Middle Ages, when power became more sophisticated and more remote from immediate contact with individual people, the *control* over supply and demand began to represent power in more recent times. Those who controlled agriculture, those who controlled large stretches of land, became the carriers of wordly power. The United States Government has played god over the years by supplying farm subsidies or buying up farm surpluses in order to increase the farmers' take. This allowed the government to put pressure on the farmers and was reflected in their votes.

Food shapes the character of an entire people. The staple food of the Far East has always been rice. The Chinese live and die on rice diets, having precious little meat, and yet they survive. But the

rice-based diet of the Chinese and other Far East-
ern nationalities has created many passive people,
people often devoid of much individuality and not
given to aggression or non-conformist attitudes.
The Japanese diet, on the other hand, based only
partially on rice, but much more on fish, a protein
food, has molded that nation's average representative into a very industrious, hard-working and
fairly aggressive individual. The largely carbohy-
drate diet of the Italian has made him into a heavy-
set, lethargic and yet very impulsive individual,
just as the high protein diet derived from animal
sources has made the average American, especially
the mid-continental type of American, into a physically strong, self-assertive, aggressive individual,
given to a great deal of power display and very little passivity. "You are what you eat" is not an
empty phrase. Taken on an individual basis, it may
not work in every case; but taken on an average
basis, by nation, it certainly does show that charac-
teristics of large groups depend upon the type of
food most common among that group.

"Man may have heart attacks because he was
born to be a vegetarian but decided to eat meat,"
three Brooklyn researchers said recently. Man's digestive system simply cannot handle the fats in
meats, the researchers theorize. The fats are depo-
sited in the walls of the arteries until the blood ves-
sels clog up. Meat-eating animals do not have the
same trouble, Drs. William S. Coleens and Efstra-
tios Vlahos say in an article on vegetarianism published recently by *Town and Country* magazine.
Dr. Collens is quoted as saying that he was so certain of the bad effects of meat, that he would not

swallow any. If he does have meat, he merely chews it and spits it out.

What food does to man in a physical sense is quite obvious. The chemical agents, incidentally, which attack the incoming food and drink supplies, extract their essences, and forward them to the appropriate body organs, are called *enzymes*. The entire endocrinal apparatus is affected in man, however, that is the system of glands and ducts which is the chemical parallel to the arterial-venous blood supply system. This is not a medical textbook so I shan't go into the details of how the essences of foodstuffs are utilized within the body, but the purely physical system of distribution is paralleled by an etheric system in which the etheric essences of foodstuffs are also sent to the proper places inside the etheric body.

If popular superstition referred to fish as "brain food," this was perhaps not entirely fictitious. The physical essence of the fish protein did not nourish the brain cells, but the etheric counterpart of it influences the etheric brain and thus directly contributes to the strengthening of the mind, which operates the etheric brain as well as the physical one, of course. But even the etheric counterpart represents tangible structures; although this structure is of a very fine substance, it has three-dimensional existence the way thoughts have three-dimensional existence in the dimension to which they belong.

Beyond these two facets of food and drink lies a third aspect, the emotional absorption of what we take in. Since food and drink stimulates our taste buds either favorably or adversely, feelings of pleasure or distaste inevitably follow. If the food we eat stimulates a sense of pleasure within us, we respond emotionally by feeling elated, satisfied, joyful, proud or any range of positive feelings. The exact level of expression differs naturally with the individual and with the particular food causing the reaction. Conversely, the opposite may be true. Negative impressions due to food can also create negative emotional responses.

Certain foods produce certain emotional fantasies; for instance, a glass of Italian wine together with a piece of cheese may create an image of a vacation in southern Europe, or a hearty steak may transport the eater into the heart of England. The responses are individual and differ greatly, but some sort of emotional reaction is produced by the intake of food. We should accept this aspect of eating and drinking and make sure that the emotional tieup with the particular food or drink is a pleasurable one.

Much of this depends upon our attitudes towards the foods we eat, of course. I should think that very few people would be particularly overjoyed at the sight of squirming wormlike water animals, eel-like creatures thrashing about in the shallow waters of the Mediterranean; yet they will eat the same creatures when they are offered to them as "fruit of the sea" and consider them a particular delicacy because they have been programmed to consider them as such. As a matter of fact the whole concept of eating meat rests very largely upon closing one's rational eyes to some pretty unpleasant facts about meat, in order to partake of it. But of this more later.

Lastly, we should consider what the absence of food and drink would do to man, if it were continued on a prolonged basis. For the absence of food and drink for short periods is not only without injurious effect to man but actually wholesome. An occasional fast of a day or half a day purifies the system and allows us to recover from the toxic attacks every one of us is subjected to in civilized society. If food is denied the body for prolonged periods, either by accident, by circumstances or willfully, the body draws upon reserves existing in the system. As a result, fatty substances stored away towards such a contingency are used up gradually, taking perhaps as much as several weeks to disappear, depending upon the individual, of course.

Man can go much longer without solid food than he can without drink. The absence of all liquids can finish him off in a span of two or three days, depending upon the climate. People have gone without solid food for weeks at a time and survived. However, if man channels his energies prudently and avoids physical expenditure of energy as much as possible, he can continue to exist on very little or no food for long periods of time. Indian Fakirs have demonstrated this over and over again, allowing themselves to be buried in nearly airtight compartments, totally cut off from food and even drink.

One note of caution, however: anyone deliberately reducing the intake of food and drink drastically over long periods of time or altogether over short periods, and then resuming a near normal or normal level, should not do so immediately since the stomach and other reception centers in the body adjust to the intake and must be given an opportunity to readjust when the intake is increased again.

If man wants to live in a material world then, he must eat and drink. If he is what he eats, he must be doubly careful that the intake of food and drink is of a constructive kind. Food and drink can materially influence not only his physical well being, but his spiritual and emotional makeup as well. Proper foods influence his future, in the sense that they can either increase or decrease his life force, his essential powers. Anyone seriously concerned with his place in life, with an improved future from the status he presently occupies, should think in terms of taking a hard look at the food and drink he takes in. He may well find that by correcting his intake of food and drink he can influence his fortunes in the future.

CHAPTER TWO
THE VEGETARIAN CREDO

Vegetarianism means a way of life based primarily on vegetable souces, that is, foods derived from vegetation. The word *vegetable* is derived from the same source, as is oddly enough, *to vegetate*, meaning *to barely get along*. This does not mean that anyone eating only vegetables is just barely alive; it means that someone may get along on a modest diet, for meat and fish have always been considered a higher form of nutrition than vegetables. This view goes back to the beginning of mankind when the primary foods were those that the hunter or fisherman brought home. In the Middle Ages meat was considered necessary for the nutrition of the soldiers, while vegetables were sufficient for women and children. Even as far back as the Stone Age the significance of meat as food was instinctively understood. A priest intent on purifying himself for some religious purpose would abstain from meat for any number of days or hours. He would not neces-

sarily abstain from all foods. Even today, those who
practice the modern version of the Stone Age Religion called the Old Religion, the people who follow
the path of Wicca, will not eat red meat or any
meat at all forty-eight hours prior to a ritual. This
was done for a twofold purpose: foregoing the pleasure of meat eating and at the same time purifying
the body by removing the substances fed into it
through the use of meat. Even then man dimly understood that meat brought certain alien substances which were not always in the best interests
of man. Today we understand that the adrenalin
released at the moment of death in the body of the
animal about to be slaughtered may be detrimental
to the health of man when he eats the meat. There
are, of course, other side effects, mainly chemical in
nature, to the consumption of meat.

In antiquity, the consumption of meat varied according to the society in which man lived. Quite obviously, an agricultural society with plenty of
grains and vegetables, would have less use or need
for meat than a society totally without agricultural
products, such as the nomadic tribes of the Arabian
Peninsula. We have to differentiate here between a
nationwide attitude towards the eating of meat—
which was rare in antiquity—and the personal, individual prohibition of meat products by sophisticated individuals for various reasons, ranging from
health to philosophy. As far as societies, entire peo-
ples, abstaining from meat in antiquity is concerned, there were none in the Western World, that
is to say Europe and Asia Minor. But in the East,
early Buddhist and Hindu societies prohibited the
use of meat altogether, couching whatever health
reasons they may have had in religious terms. Par-

tial prohibition of meat existed a very long time ago in the Near East, pertaining particularly to meat derived from animals considered unclean, such as pork.

In the East, the attitude of Buddhist and Hindu societies has remained the same 2000 years later, even though individual members may no longer practice the strict prescriptions of their religion. Likewise, Semitic societies in the Near East still frown upon the consumption of pork and pork products. But again, the orthodox element obeys the law while the progressive element frequently does not. In the West, meaning Europe and the European colonies in the New World, vegetarianism on religious grounds did not exist on any large-scale basis. There were, however, small religious splinter groups, such as the Seventh Day Adventists, who preached a religious vegetarianism based upon the sanctity of all life. To this day the Seventh Day Adventists societies adhere to this belief and practice it. But by and large, the upsurge of vegetarianism in the Western World is the product of 19th century emancipation and a humane outlook on the part of individuals, who then became the spiritual and intellectual leaders of the vegetarian movement and in turn spread their philosophies to larger segments of the population. There was no deep seated, "grass roots" movement for vegetarianism prevalent in Europe prior to the second half of the 19th century, although individual poets and writers may at times have pointed out the horrors of slaughter and the dangers of meat. Probably the most prominent of these writers is the late George Bernard Shaw. Throughout his life he admonished his fellow man to forego the use of meat, both on moral and on health grounds. He predicted blandly that he would live to a ripe old age, and when he finally died, his coffin would be followed by a procession of various farm animals whose lives he had saved by abstaining from eating their meat. As it happened, Shaw died in his mid-nineties, and never suffered any great debilitating illnesses during his long life. Shavian vegetarianism is pretty much the most common form of this philosophy in the Western World today.

Essentially there are three types of vegetarians, and three motivations for being a vegetarian. The three types of vegetarian are the Vegan, the Lactarian and the Ovo-lactarian. The Vegan and his variant, the Fructarian, abstains from all animals, animal products, eggs and milk products, even from the use of vitamins and additives, and lives therefore mainly on vegetables, fruits and nuts. Vegans are firmly convinced that any form of processed food is detrimental and prefer their food raw, whenever that is possible, rather than cooked. They maintain that sufficient vitamins are contained in the vegetables they eat so that vitamin pills are not necessary for the diet.

Dr. Jean Mayer in his article in *Family Health* says, "There are large numbers of our contemporaries who seem to have become vegetarians out of fear. The Vegans in England who avoid all animal products are apparently motivated largely by the belief that animal products cause cancer. In this country there is a somewhat more sophisticated belief, that meat and poultry are full of hormones which will cause cancer. Fish is said to be preserved in antibiotics, which will sap your ability to fend off germs, milk is full of DDT, and eggs are saturated with mysterious unnamed chemicals. Not one of these claims is true, but all of the proof in the world can't seem to change the attitude of this type of vegetarian about animal foods."

Since this article appeared in February 1973, one can only assume Mayer was ignorant of statements an article in *The New York Times* of September 29, 1972, headlined, "Dietary Factors Linked to Cancer of Digestive Tract." In this special article by Jane E. Brody, it is stated that, "Worldwide changes in the incidence of cancers of the digestive tract are pointing to meats, alcohol and a deficiency of the trace element molybdenum in the diet as possible causes of these major cancer killers. Dr. John W. Berg, epidemiologist at the National Cancer Institute, told the Seventh National Cancer Conference, 'Much to our surprise, six different meat items were found to be associated with a high bowel cancer risk' and he explained that Argentina and Scotland, which use a lot of meat, have high bowel cancer rates not much different from that in the United States. He is quoted as emphasizing that this did not mean that eating meat caused bowel cancer, but it would mean that something in the meat or added to it was the culprit. At present, the doctor explained, science had no explanation for any such causative relationship. Studies are now being conducted among vegetarians, who eat no meat, and Seventh Day Adventists, who eat little meat, to seek further confirmation of his findings."

That unwanted or unneeded hormones can cause cancer in humans is well known among doctors. And it is a fact that much meat and poultry in the United States is being injected with hormones, in order to make the meat more valuable. It is also a fact that these hormones go right into the human body with the consumption of such meats. Dr. Mayer makes light of the fear by British Vegans that milk may contain DDT, but it is also a fact that DDT has also been outlawed in the United States for that very reason. Animals eating grass sprayed previously with DDT, or for that matter with any other insecticide, store the poison in their system and it does go into the milk and thence into the human body. Not only are these claims or fears rational but they do not even cover the entire range of dangers existing in the consumption of meat or fish products.

However, Vegans are by no means representative of the majority of vegetarians in the world today. They are, in a sense, the conservatives among vegetarians, preferring a very strict diet to one of convenience. The majority of vegetarians is either Lactarian, meaning they partake of milk products, or *Ovo-lactarian*, meaning they partake of milk and egg products. I myself am a Lactarian: I eat cheeses and milk products but I do not eat eggs or egg products.

Those who are Lactarians like myself find that their diet is well-balanced and generally there is enough of a variety of foods available to them so that no problem of nutrition exists. This is even more the case with Ovo-lactarians. Since the majority of desserts, for instance, contain eggs, and since eggs are added to a number of other dishes as well, an honest Lactarian or Vegan will not touch a piece of pastry containing eggs, even if one egg has been used in 500 lbs. of pastry. It is not the amount of the unwanted product that counts but the principle behind it.

Both Lactarians and Ovo-lactarians take vitamins with their food although they insist on the vitamins being of natural or organic origin. In cities especially, the need for additives such as vitamins is particularly great. However, if one lives in the open country and has access to fresh vegetables or even grows one's own, vitamins are no longer required in most cases. This is so because the vegetables coming onto the market in the city are generally two to three days old, by which time the vitamin content has either shrunk or been completely eliminated. Only freshly cut vegetables or freshly collected fruit maintain the high vitamin content originally put into them by nature.

The majority of vegetarians, who are either Lactarians or Ovo-lactarians, are also interested in health foods and will buy their products at health food stores, although it must be remembered that health food and vegetarianism are two different things. Likewise, faddish diets such as the macrobiotic diet have nothing to do with real vegetarianism. The macrobiotic diet, formulated by a Japanese school of philosophy in recent years, consists primarily of selected fish products and some vegetables. It differentiates between that which is grown close to the ground and that which grows above ground. Ultimately more and more foods are eliminated from the system until the dieter lives on brown rice alone. While such a diet may be suitable to some selected individuals living a quiet contemplative life in the Far East, it is totally unsuitable and perhaps even dangerous to a Westerner. I have seen people try the macrobiotic diet for a number of months, until their health was in such a poor state that they had to discontinue it. Some of the reasoning behind the prohibition of certain vegetables seems unwarranted. More than anything, the macrobiotic diet is an implementation of a religious belief and not based on health motivation or on moral concepts. It is closely associated with Zen Buddhism.

There seems to be some question in the mind of the outside observer concerning the prohibition of eggs and egg products by some vegetarians. The argument goes like this: An egg is not an animal, especially an unfertilized egg. Why should it not be consumed? The answer of course is that an egg does represent a comparatively high stage of development towards animal life, whether fertilized or not, and while eating an unfertilized egg does not deprive a chicken of its potential life, it does in fact represent the consumption of an animal-like product, made up of materials similar to the chicken itself once it is born.

To this, many will reply: But what about milk and cheese, are they not also derived from animals? They most certainly are, but the cow giving milk not only continues a happy life but is relieved by giving up the milk, since she has too much, and not enough calves to feed. Certainly, if the breeding of farm animals for slaughter were to be discontinued, milk would no longer be freely available, for then cows would need it to feed their own. Until such time however, milk is available in abundance and should be utilized for human consumption. Cheeses are generally made in a natural way from the milk. Process cheeses are not very much liked by most vegetarians for other reasons; if they are at all interested in health food standards, they know that processing destroys most values in the cheese.

There are people who consider themselves vegetarians when in fact they are not. I am referring here to those who eat fish but not meat or poultry or those who eat meat only once a week perhaps or only when they are in company to avoid standing out. That kind of vegetarianism is laughable; a diet which permits one to go off it whenever one so decides is not a diet at all but an indulgence.

The fallacy that fish meat is less undesirable than meat derived from beef or poultry from the vegetarian point of view is another myth; neither is fish meat any less poisoned than other meat, since our rivers and lakes are polluted; and while a fish may not have a voice to cry out against being killed, its anxiety at the moment of death is just as great as a farm animal's capable of venting its fears. Thus the problem of adrenalin accumulated just before the moment of death, comes as much into play with fish as with other forms of meat. This applies equally to seafood, crustaceans and, in fact, any kind of animal meat, whether of a higher or lower order.

It does not apply to plants being ripped from the soil or cut off because plants have a different kind of organism, devoid of blood, and do not respond the way animals do. But in terms of taking life, of course, plants do represent a life force also, and if one were to carry vegetarianism to extremes, one would not eat salads or vegetables, but live only off fruit and nuts, since these two categories alone permit the host, that is the tree, to function after the fruit or nut has been taken, without harm to the host organism. The truly perfect vegetarian, therefore, is not the Vegan, but the Fruitarian, a person who eats only raw fruits and nuts and nothing else. A diet based on these two categories can be entirely sufficient, but is very difficult to maintain in organized society.

We have seen that there are three types of vegetarians, and at least two types of non-vegetarians who sometimes claim that distinction. When it comes to the motivating factor, there are three lines of thought behind being a vegetarian. First of all, there is the religious concept. The deity prohibits the intake of food derived from living beings.

I have already pointed out that Buddhists and Hindus alike prohibit meat for similar although not identical reasons. The Buddhist will not partake of meat because he believes in transmigration of the soul. He accepts the possibility that man may be reincarnated in the body of an animal, and it is therefore unwise to eat animals because one never knows whom one is eating. The Hindu, practicing the Vedic Religion, will not kill cows because Shiva, the principal deity of the Hindu pantheon, is always represented on a bull, and bull and cow are sacred to Shiva. Consequently, the streets of some Indian cities are even today clogged with cows leading a peaceful and pampered existence because no one dares kill them or even push them out of the way.

Less direct, but just as religious, is Western man's belief that God loves all his creations, including his animals, equally as well as he loves man. Therefore, this religiously-oriented vegetarian argues, it is not right for man to take advantage of his fellow creatures by eating them. Such great humanitarians as Albert Schweitzer, who proclaimed the sanctity of all life, are among those who practiced vegetarianism. Some extremely devout Christians will not eat meat either, especially among the more restricted orders, such as the Carmelites.

Large numbers of Christian laymen will not eat meat on Friday—any Friday—and especially not during the "passion" of Christ around Easter. The belief that the abstention from meat atones for the sins of the flesh perpetrated against Jesus is behind this attitude. In medieval Spain and Italy the consumption of meat was somehow connected with the sins of the flesh, in that abstention from meat also meant abstention from the pleasures of the flesh. Yet, most languages have two separate words for animal meat and human meat, flesh. A glaring exception is German, but then Germany was largely Protestant from the 16th century onward, and the identification of meat eating with sins of the flesh was primarily a Catholic viewpoint. Only in the later Protestant movements, notably 18th century Puritanism, does the identification of meat with flesh reoccur. Whether Catholic or Protestant, the prohibitions against the consumption of meat, of alcoholic beverages or of partaking in pleasures of the flesh were also intended to deprive the believer of the joy involved. Joy was something the religious philosophers of the time did not like, preferring that man repent instead and turn his thoughts inward towards purification of the soul, and denial of the body as far as possible.

In whatever religion, sacrificing an animal had nothing to do with the flesh of the animal; it was the life that was being offered in sacrifice, not the body of the victim. In those religions where the priesthood would then partake of the flesh of the sacrificed animal, such as in Egypt, that was done as a transcendental expression of partaking of the deity itself. Since the meat belonged to the deity once it had been sacrificed, eating the meat forged an immediate link between deity and priesthood.

Vegetarians in all three categories make a great deal of the presence of blood in animals. The reason vegetarians do not consider the eating of plants in the same category as the consumption of animals is because plants do not have blood. Blood is thought to be the carrier of the life force. Even in the use of the term in our language, we speak of "shedding someone's blood," or of "pure blood." Many misguided individuals object to blood transfusions because they can't be sure that the blood they might receive in an emergency would not come from a racially different individual, as if the color of blood would differ with the color of the races whence it came.

"Blood is a very special juice" Goethe has his Mephistopheles warn Faust in the drama of the same name. The alleged compacts between witches and the devil were always signed in blood. Blood is the very essence of beginning life, as in women's menstruation and the placenta at birth. When a religiously oriented vegetarian rejects meat because it contains blood he is therefore on very good philosophical ground.

Substituting wine for blood in the Christian service is another way of suggesting that instead of a sacrifice, meaning the spilling of blood, the fruits of the land should be used. As the cereal of the communion service replaces the body of Christ so does the wine eliminate the need for a blood sacrifice. To the Pagan, a number of animals could not be killed and eaten for food because they were sacred to certain deities. The stag was of course sacred to Diana, the huntress. The Christian hunter had similar misgivings. Did not a sacred stag appear to St. Hubert? When it came to breeding farm animals, things were not as bad. Of course, the Pagan might remember that Pan was a goat headed god and that the goat was sacred to him, and the Christians might consider Jesus' claim to be the Lamb of God, whenever they would partake of the meat of the sheep. On the other hand, however, early Christians, living underground during the time of Roman persecutions, would consume fish whenever they could simply because the Greek word for fish, *ichthys*, also represented the initials Jesus.

Vegetarianism on moral grounds is perhaps the most common of all. One motivation does not necessarily exclude another, but not every vegetarian objects to the eating of meat on health grounds alone. In a way, that would be a selfish reason but being morally against the eating of meat also implies being against the killing of animals for the purpose of obtaining their meat. Thus, morally motivated vegetarians are generally anti-war, anti-violence and pro-humanitarian. Such vegetarians feel that animals were not put on this earth to serve us as food but to share in the use and enjoyment of nature.

It is comparatively easy to be a humanitarian vegetarian, if one lives in a small town or village and becomes personally acquainted with the farm animals about to be slaughtered. It is even easier to turn vegetarian when one watches them being slaughtered, for man has as yet not devised an easy way of dispatching the unfortunate victims of his avarice, even though technology has made it seem so. In a society in which slaughterhouses are mechanically operated and usually not accessible to average people, the very remoteness of the final process itself makes it a little easier on the meat eater to accept the situation. I should think that the majority of those who eat meat do not realize how the meat is obtained or what agonies the animals undergo just prior to slaughter, but the fact remains, animals are raised for the sole purpose of murder. They may even be given a degree of love and attention, only to make them grow better and thus provide their owners with more food. This in itself is a morally objectionable process; it is a little like deceiving the animal, fostering its belief that it is being cared for when in fact it is being prepared for death all along.

Animals do not do such things to other animals. It is true that some animals live on the meat of other animals, while others do not, being complete vegetarians. But animals who kill other animals do so only when they need to, and there is never any insidious preparation, but sudden attack. Man, on the other hand, breeds his animals slowly and carefully, creating an entire industry for the sole purpose of encouraging life in his fellow creatures in order to snuff it out at will, without those creatures having any say or a chance to fight back. There is a great deal of difference between the hunting of wild animals and the breeding of livestock for the purpose of slaughter. While hunting itself is objectionable as a sport, the killing of a wild animal for food may at times be excused if no other food supply is available: it then becomes an act of survival; but the deliberate breeding of livestock for slaughter is more in the nature of premeditated murder, and from the moralist's point of view far more objectionable.

To the vegetarian who rejects meat on moral grounds, there is no difference between the eating of meat derived from animals and that of people. To him, cannibals are just as logical as meat eaters. As a matter of fact, so are cannibals to themselves. In the few primitive societies surviving today where cannibalism is still being practiced occasionally, the explanation is always: in partaking of the flesh of an enemy or superior individual one derives the strength of that individual and fuses it with one's own. In a way, the primitive cannibal considers it an honor for his victim to be eaten. If he were not worthy of being eaten, the cannibal wouldn't have bothered. Incidentally, comic strips to the contrary, cannibals do not boil their intended victims in cauldrons over open fires, but kill them as humanely as possible within the context of their primitive societies. By contrast we should remember the unfortunate custom still in existence in some areas of boiling crustaceans alive in order to make them more tender.

People who accept the reality of reincarnation also know that taking another man's life brings inevitable retribution. Karmic law must be fulfilled; the taking of another person's life will result in some misfortune in one's own, or one wrong must be rectified by doing something right in another area. But the majority of meat eaters never give it much thought that animals may have spirits as well and that killing them may create another kind of Karmic debt for them. The vegetarian has no such problem; he is free from all guilt when it comes to the taking of life of animals.

The third reason why people become vegetarians has to do with health. Long before pollution, DDT, and other food additives became a problem and subject to public discussion, vegetarians felt that the intake of secondary foodstuffs, which, after all, meat represents, was detrimental to the system. They felt that it was wiser to obtain one's food supplies from primary sources such as vegetables, nuts and fruits. Meat represents a secondary source in that the animal eats vegetables, fruit and nuts in order to live. The problem with secondary food sources is that one inherits all the diseases and weaknesses of that source as well.

Of course, there are other factors. Meat has to be broken down in the system and requires far more effort to eat than plants. Meat also brought with it direct additions to man's protein and blood supplies, thus unbalancing the natural amount present in the system. Plants can be utilized in the human body in many ways; with meats, a highly organized food product, utilization can only go in a small number of directions. As a result of this, meat eaters tend to take in too much protein, causing adverse reactions in both body and mind. Since farm animals are not always very clean, other impurities enter the bloodstream of the meat eater through the medium of the meat. With pork in particular, the danger of infection through such diseases as trichinosis, or tapeworm, is always present. As man is not particularly choosy as to which part of the animal's body he will eat, especially if his economic status makes it difficult for him to have the choice sections, areas of the animal will enter the consumer's body that are not meant to be eaten at all, such as the insides and eliminative organs of the animals.

There is another health factor not always realized by even avid vegetarians. By the intake of meat, the non-vegetarian also takes on the etheric counterpart of the animal's body. With it comes the accumulated anxiety prior to slaughter; illness may result from this alone. Of course, no butcher will ever accept the possibility that his animals have an inner or etheric body as well. He cannot sell it, consequently he has no use for it. But the possibility seems indicated that the etheric body of the animal is not necessarily freed at the time of slaughter, but may hang on to the physical counterpart or portions of the physical counterpart for some time before being able to break loose and enter into the non-physical dimension. We know as yet very little about this aspect of animal afterlife but the meat eater very definitely is in danger of acquiring etheric components of a disturbing nature whenever he eats freshly slaughtered meat.

"A great many vegetarians nowadays are not motivated by religious precepts but by simple compassion for our fellow creatures. Carnivorous animals must kill to survive, but we are omnivorous; we can replace meat with other sources of protein. Therefore we do not need to be part of the killing" says Dr. Jean Mayer. After sounding a warning that milk and milk products are necessary to children and mothers, if they are not to suffer in later years, Dr. Mayer observes, "We have found that a number of young persons who have recently abandoned the use of hard drugs go through a long period, a year or more, of vegetarianism. Whether this is done as a health measure for their purification or as a testimony to their continuing membership in the counterculture, we are not sure. The preparation of elaborate vegetable diets, eschewing all convenience foods, often seems to provide the only organized activity in an otherwise footloose existence."

Although I lecture before young audiences most of the time, I have found no connection between the drug culture and an interest in vegetarianism. I have, however, found that those who are interested in ESP, the occult, astrology or witchcraft, frequently evince an equal interest in vegetarianism. If anything, the peace-loving, establishment-doubting element among the young finds that a vegetarian way of life fits them best. In a way, they can express their hatred of all violence by abstaining from violating animals, but in the many cases familiar to me this has come about by a gradual process of learning and enlightenment—not as a result of abandoning the use of drugs.

What is a vegetarian? Twenty years ago a vegetarian was a man, usually bearded, who walked the streets wearing strange clothes, had an unkempt fanatical look about him and quite obviously did not belong to the mainstream of society. Vegetarians were oddballs, rebels, weirdos. For some time there was a vegetarian party, headed by the editor of a small vegetarian journal, which attempted to place their candidate in Congress. But the Vegetarian Party did not succeed any more than the Townsend Party succeeded in placing their pension reform candidate into the White House. Political vegetarianism is dead. Fanatical vegetarians are comparatively few in number: middle-of-the-road vegetarians exist by the millions.

In addition to the three reasons given above, some people who do not believe in being vegetarian become vegetarians because it suits them at a given time. This may be in order to lose weight, or in order to streamline their physical appearance or in order to strengthen their state of health. They are vegetarians for a time and then return to being meat eaters or they do it because it is an "in" fad or to please someone they love. A vegetarian, then, is someone who does not eat meats or meat products, nor fish nor fish products and, in the majority of cases, no eggs or egg products. If he is a total abstainer from all animal products, including milk and milk products, he is referred to as a Vegan or if he abstains from all plant products except fruits and nuts, as a Fructarian. The latter kind are very rare in this country simply because it is very difficult to maintain a healthy life in a rapidly moving society such as ours with fruit and nuts as sole sources of the diet. Certainly a person who eats fish but no meat is not a vegetarian and a person who eats meat rarely is not a vegetarian. Nor is a person following the Jewish dietary laws a vegetarian even though Jews have some parallel restrictions such as the prohibition of pork and pork products. Whatever the motivation, a vegetarian is, or should be, an individual living a balanced life—if anything, in better health than his fellow man partaking of meat; more peaceful and understanding than his meat eating cousin; and on the whole, a more advanced person than the non-vegetarian.

Vegetarian Guidelines

1. I shall not eat the meat, or meat products derived from animals, whether large or small, whether flesh, fowl or fish.
2. I shall not use products containing chemical agents likely to hurt my state of health.
3. I shall not destroy the food I use by overcooking, but eat whatever is palatable and digestible in its raw state.
4. I shall not drink alcoholic beverages (with the exception of small amounts of wine or wine-derived drinks occasionally), and I

shall not smoke or use drugs at any time.

5. I shall attempt to clothe myself without the use of leather, to discourage the use of animal skins for clothing and shoes.

6. I shall always remember that mine is a peaceful Way of Life and not to impose it on others, no matter what, unless they wish to embrace it.

CHAPTER THREE

WHY I BECAME A VEGETARIAN

I was born into an upper middle-class family of urban Austria, the son of a returnee from New York who had gone to America at the tender age of 14 to find his fortune. Unfortunately, my father did not have enough time to find his fortune when his own father fell ill and required his presence in Austria. My father returned to Vienna and did not set foot again on American soil for more than thirty years. In the interim, he married and had two children, the younger of which was I. From the very beginning, and as far back as I can remember, I was a rebel—but one with a cause.

As with every family, there are children who don't want to eat at certain times or certain foods. (In my case, spinach was not to my liking. But I ate my spinach, simply because I had to.) At the age of six, when I was already in the second grade of grammar school, I began to develop a strange distaste for the meat of animals. Even earlier than that I remember refusing venison when it was brought to the table. We lived in the city, and the meat of wild animals was not part of our ordinary diet, but on one rare occasion someone had given my parents part of a deer, and it had been prepared with all the trimmings. The time was Christmas, and the festive mood was somewhat shattered by my absolute refusal to eat that type of meat. I explained to my parents that I couldn't stand the particular smell of wild animal's meat. Although my parents were not terribly strict disciplinarians, they felt that good food should be eaten whether or not the child liked it. However, my insistence that I would not eat it was just as strong. The matter was abandoned and an omelet was substituted. My older brother, incidentally, had no such problems. He ate whatever was put before him and to this day he is the easiest person to please when it comes to food. But my parents realized that venison was out as far as I was concerned.

Soon there was an occasion to reject fish. I explained this on the grounds that I was afraid of having a bone stuck in my throat. My mother therefore patiently pulled all the little bones from the fish and then presented it to me. I still didn't eat it. But I did eat veal, beef, and chicken. I would not touch any of the fatty parts nor would I eat the insides of animals, such as heart, liver or other organs. I would turn in horror when someone ate calves brains, and I would not touch anything but the leanest portions of the three principal meat dishes.

On one occasion, I recall being at my grandmother's house in Czechoslovakia, when duck was being served. I wouldn't touch it, even after my grandmother and my uncles pointed out to me that there was very little difference between a chicken and a duck. Something within me made me cringe whenever any unfamiliar meat was being served. As yet I managed with the three principal meat types and with sausage. I did eat eggs and as a matter of fact, loved omelets.

At age 11 I was sent to Switzerland for one summer. While I was at school in Vevey, I had a rather upsetting experience. On the second day of my arrival I was introduced to the rest of the boys in the dining room. The place was rather noisy. The atmosphere was frantic. Lunch was being served, and a dish was put before me, without my having had a chance to discuss what I wanted to eat. While I was still examining the dish before me, one of the older boys came over and unceremoniously took some of the food from my plate. Somehow this wanton act made the food even less desirable; as it was, it turned out to be calves liver, something I wouldn't have eaten anyway.

The four weeks in Switzerland were most difficult, as far as food was concerned. I avoided any dishes containing foods I couldn't eat, explaining my revulsion against them. My teachers shrugged; it didn't matter to them so long as I ate something and learned my lessons. When my father came to fetch me at the end of the summer, I couldn't wait to tell him what I had decided. "I'm not going to eat meat anymore," I said in a firm voice as soon as we had a moment to ourselves. My father looked at me in astonishment, asking me to explain. I repeated the statement, adding that I had come to the conclusion that the eating of animals' meat was wrong, and at any rate wrong for me and I would no longer do so. My father pleaded with me, explaining that I would endanger my health if I didn't have a balanced diet. More to appease him than because I was in agreement I assured him that I would continue to eat eggs and sausage, which I somehow considered less objectionable than meat. Perhaps this was so because there is no blood visible with sausage or eggs, while meat frequently has some of the original blood of the animal still in it.

After I had arrived at our home, I had just a few days before packing again and going to my grandmother's house for the rest of the season. The very first night of my arrival in Czechoslovakia, I startled my family by telling them about my diet. That night, duck was the big treat. I refused it. I refused meat the following day. By the third day my grandmother gave in. I could have whatever I wanted. As yet I found I could eat eggs, especially omelets. So for the following years I lived on a diet of vegetables, fruits, nuts and some eggs and sausage. By the time I was 14, I realized that sausage was a form of meat and abruptly stopped it. Only eggs remained part of my diet from that moment on.

It wasn't until I lived in New York City in the middle fifties, that I stopped eating eggs altogether. One day I looked at an egg and realized how close it was to a fertilized egg and life itself. From that moment on omelets disappeared from my menu. Even desserts containing small amounts of egg were on the forbidden list.

To this day, I've kept to my philosophy. I have not touched a single piece of meat, fish, or eggs or products containing any of these substances, although I drink milk and eat cheeses. More and more, as time goes on, I veer towards the use of health foods exclusively, or at any rate to the extent I am able to find them. My diet is balanced, my intake is normal, and I am at peace with my environment.

To be sure, I did not react with horror when others at the same table ate meat. Whenever anyone asked me whether it bothered me to see them eating meat, especially bloody meat, I shrugged, explaining that I did not care what others did, so long as no one tried to interfere with my beliefs. Actually, the strong smell of fish has always caused me nausea, not so much because of moral considerations, but perhaps due to a natural allergy against that particular smell. I have also found the peculiar scent of wild animal meat offensive. However, I never tried to convince others of going my way.

As time went on, I was asked to attend various functions. To tell a prospective dinner host or hostess that one does not eat fish, meat, eggs, or products containing them, is a difficult task. On the one hand, telling them of one's peculiarity saves trouble. On the other hand, it puts one into a difficult position as if one were ordering in a restaurant. Consequently I was always torn between telling them or playing it by ear, remarking rather lightly that I would be fine eating just the vegetables and never mind about the rest.

I remember one occasion when I was invited to a state function, a dinner party given by the then French ambassador to Austria in his official residence. I was in Vienna as a writer and U.S. foreign correspondent and had become friendly with the French cultural attaché. I did not dare tell my prospective hosts about being a vegetarian. After we were seated at the dinner table, I was offered various meat dishes which I had to decline. Since the number of guests was very small, no more than a dozen, this was a little difficult. I did the trick by turning to my right-hand neighbor whenever I was being served from the left and my left-hand neighbor whenever I was being served from the right. I almost got away with it, just eating a few vegetables and potatoes, but the sharp eye of the ambassador's wife could not help but notice my peculiar behavior. Afterwards, she asked me and I told her. "Why on earth didn't you tell me before," she thundered. In punishment I had to come back for lunch the following Sunday, so that she could cook me a real vegetarian meal of her own choosing. It was one of the most delicious meals I've ever had.

Once in a while a hostess will go to elaborate trouble to have a special dish for me, only to discover that eggs are out as far as I am concerned. Somehow it rarely occurs to people that eggs might be on the forbidden list of a vegetarian. But they are, in my case, and I keep to my philosophy, whether or not the amount of egg is large or small. Frequently, people will say, "But eat it just this once. What is the difference? "The difference is that I have arrived at a philosophy of life after many years of thinking it out, and it either works all the time or it doesn't work at all. When oneself is the judge of one's actions, the judgment is bound to be just.

A tolerant person not only expects tolerance from others for his particular point of view, but he must be prepared to extend tolerance even in areas that may entail a certain amount of discomfort. On several occasions before I was married, I would entertain people who were very definitely meat eaters. Although I had very little experience in cooking, I prepared steak dinner for them, overcoming my own revulsion, by suggesting to myself that I was, after all, doing this for someone else and that it did not matter. I understand the steaks were quite good; at least, nobody complained.

My wife is not a vegetarian but she eats little meat; her mother, on the other hand, was a full vegetarian for many years and yet did not try to influence her daughter to join her way of life. My older daughter Nadine, now 10 years of age, did not have a single bite of meat or fish until age three; for the first three years of her life, she was given only vegetarian food, with a strong accent on health foods. She is one of the strongest and healthiest children in her class, the tallest, and though she began to eat meat after age three, the foundation was laid on vegetarian food. I think it is as wrong to force one's own philosophy on others, including one's children, as it is to allow oneself to be forced to give in to convention or convenience in such matters. Everyone must do their own thing, as they see it. So long as it doesn't harm anyone, there is no need to conform.

No one needs to defend his vegetarianism. On the few occasions where people questioned my judgment in this matter, wondering why on earth I would want to be a vegetarian, I have rather sharply, even if politely, reminded them that being a meat eater was merely a different point of view. No one needs to defend himself for being vegetarian. If anything, it will be the meat eaters in the long run who will have to defend their way of life, for as time goes on medical science discovers more and more evidence that meat eating is detrimental to health.

Whenever meat was being cooked or served, I found the sight of it at the very least unpleasant, at times revolting. Seeing the form of an animal on the plate, or part of an animal's body dissected before my eyes somehow disturbed my sense of humanity. I felt that we were doing things to our animal friends we oughtn't to. Some of the animals being eaten reminded me of smaller human beings, after all, having legs and shoulders and heads. More and more I thought that the practice of killing animals and then preparing them as food was barbarous. In addition to a sense of moral indignation at the idea of eating animals came a sense of revulsion fed largely by sight values whenever I saw meat or fish. I found the idea of putting part of an animal into my mouth, chewing it, and swallowing it totally impossible. When I was a young boy and not always possessed of the best judgment in such matters, I might have made some tactless remarks to those who enjoyed meat; the result was that they didn't enjoy their meat as much as before, nor did they like me as much. Nowadays I do no such thing, for I feel that everyone must find his own way, his own path to the light as it were, his own Karmic fulfilment. But I can hold out the path to truth in such a way that it is not offensive, that there is no pressure upon them to accept it, merely an opportunity to study what I have to say.

From an early stage, my attitude towards animals was different from that of most boys of my age. While children of five or six years of age like to keep a pet at home, such as a squirrel or gerbil, or perhaps a guinea pig, they do so because the animal represents a pet, an animated pet that is different from the dolls of their early childhood or because, as a result of school, they have become fascinated with the animal kingdom and like to study it at home as well. But there's rarely a kinship with the animal they bring home or keep in cages. How can there be, when the animal is bereft of its freedom and is in the home merely to amuse its little owner? My attitude towards animals was different from the beginning. I would look out into the woods and see the birds fly about freely, squirrels running up and down trees unhampered, and I felt a deep sense of kinship with them and their sense of freedom. Perhaps because I am an Aquarian by birth, I always felt that freedom to move about was an essential part of existence, whether in man or animal. Consequently, I developed a deep-seated dislike for pet shops. When I was eight years old I would save up my allowances, and when there was enough in the piggy bank, would insist on being brought to the nearest pet shop in the company of my tutor, so that I could liberate one or the other animal imprisoned there. Generally, there was just enough money to buy some cheap bird such as a bullfinch or swallow.

Once I had enough money to go for a crossbeak, a rather large, multicolored bird, fond of eating sunflower seeds and nuts. I had gotten to know the crossbeaks in the park and woodlands of my native Austria; in the winter I would go out into the parks and feed them. Consequently I thought that liberating a crossbeak would be the best thing to do. When I arrived at the pet shop, I found I was in luck. There was a rather large crossbeak sitting in a cage, staring at me with somewhat doubting eyes. Quickly I paid for it and took the cage to the nearest woods. There, with a short speech to the bird, I put my hand inside the cage. The bird immediately bit my finger. Startled, I closed the door again. It was obvious to me that the bird had gotten accustomed to life in the pet shop and was much too old to try for a different kind of life in the woods. Sadly, I took the cage back to the pet shop and exchanged the elderly crossbeak for two young bullfinches. Hardly had I opened the door for them, when they flew out and quickly disappeared into the woods, leaving me with snatches of a bright melody and an empty cage.

The idea that animals were suffering always haunted me. During the cold winter months I established a regular route in a nearby park, nailing old cigar boxes to trees, and filled them with various sorts of bird food. At a lower level, I would install another box containing food for the squirrels. Twice a week, I would visit my route and refill the boxes. Although it was technically against the law to nail cigar boxes to trees, no policeman ever challenged my right to do so. As a result of this I got to know the birds and squirrels pretty well. Hardly would I approach a box to refill it, when the birds would swoop down from the trees and start walking up and down my arms. Squirrels would come to welcome me, sit up on their haunches and await their rations. It got so that the neighborhood grocers would set aside certain low-grade rice and other foodstuffs to be given to me free of charge for my birds and squirrels. I even built a birdhouse on my windowsill, feeding all my neighborhood crossbeaks, bullfinches, titmice, and other birds to a point where the refuse accumulating underneath my window alarmed the landlord and he put a stop to it.

Naturally, such an attitude towards animals would make it very difficult for a boy of ten or eleven years to partake of a meal of grouse or pigeon. After all, he would see in them the same things he sees in the birds in the park. To this day, I cannot conceive of interfering with the appetite of the mountain deer coming onto our property in the Austrian Alps, even though they sometimes eat the roses or some of our best salads. Somehow I feel that they have as much of a right to them as we have. When you have seen a group of deer cavorting in the early morning mist, on the mountain meadow, unafraid of man, and enjoying thoroughly their natural playfulness, you will not want to see them killed by the hunter's rifle or served up for food and you will not want to see them deprived of food in times when there isn't enough on the ground.

Anyone who has ever been to or near a slaughterhouse, especially the large slaughterhouse factories in the Middle West, will remember the stench of death that hovers over it for many miles around. There is an atmosphere loaded with tension and depression in these places, which represents the etheric energies freed in a confusing manner by the death of so many animals against their wishes. It is perhaps no accident that meat-packing communities such as Chicago and East St. Louis are also centers of criminal activity, places where men act with violence, more than at other places enjoying nature's calming and uplifting influences.

Of course, if we are to accept that animals have souls exactly the way people have, then killing them would represent a somewhat different problem. If they are only bodies provided to us by a thoughtful nature, then we need not worry about that. As it is, however, there is every evidence to point to the survival of animal spirits beyond physical death, judging from the evidence on hand in various psychical research societies. We are therefore committing the same kind of murder whether we kill a human being or an animal. The only difference is that animals have not as yet found a way of fighting back collectively, or finding refuge and protection in the law.

Naturally, plants also have an etheric counterpart, but from the available evidence plants do not suffer the way animals do when they are being torn from the earth, because of the absence of blood and of a complicated nervous system. Then, too, plants grow again the following year from the same seeds and at the same places. Animals do not get born in exactly the same fashion. When we kill and eat an animal, we have snuffed out a life. When we cut a salad green from its bed or a stalk of corn in the field, we are merely taking that year's crop, sure that another crop like it will grow the following season. The individuality of plants is much less pronounced than that of animals. Plants, by and large, are a species; animals are individual living beings.

As a vegetarian I, of course, oppose all vivisection and medical animal experiments. I do not only oppose them, but hold them to be totally unnecessary and useless. More and more medical researchers find the experiments conducted with animals do not yield the same results when the findings are applied to human beings, simply because human beings are not the same as animals and react in different ways from them. Even if animal experiments were to be condoned as a measure towards enlightenment and to save man from suffering, there would be no excuse for the many duplications of such experiments going on simultaneously at colleges and research centers throughout the world. For that reason I cannot agree with some of the practices of the American Society For the Prevention of Cruelty to Animals, especially their turning dogs and cats in their shelters over to research after a certain period of time. A vegetarian not only doesn't eat meat, he does not accept the killing of animals for any purpose other than meat eating. He does not accept the cruelty sometimes inflicted on horses and dogs; nor the imprisonment of wild birds in cages; nor hunting and fishing as a sport, without immediate need for food. All life is sacred, Albert Schweitzer stated many times. All life is indeed sacred to me, and being a vegetarian is part of that creed.

CHAPTER FOUR
HEALTH FOOD AND VEGETARIANISM

To the uninitiated there doesn't seem to be much difference, if any, between being a vegetarian and buying health foods. To the outsider, both approaches reek of the unusual, the offbeat, that "something" that lumps people into special categories. If this was excusable as the point of view of the misinformed ten or twelve years ago, when the health food movement was in its infancy, it is certainly not acceptable even from the misinformed today, since the health food industry has become a multi-million dollar business, complete with abuses and exaggerated claims like any other business.

To begin with, vegetarianism relies upon the abstinence from certain food categories. Health food users cut clear across the line from extreme meat eaters to total vegetarians. Health food is simply a food grown, processed or otherwise obtained under superior conditions than those prevailing at the ordinary food purveyors. Consequently, health food does not only include vegetables, cereals, stimulants, vitamins, nuts and fruit, but also meat, fish, eggs, and milk products. In fact, the health food industry is now at work to produce everything ordinary food producers can come up with, except, of course, under different conditions and, I might add, different prices, for the health food industry has of late become exorbitantly expensive, far beyond the requirements of the business.

It is true that the smaller the clientele, the greater the risk, but health food enthusiasts now number in the millions. Health food stores and franchises dot the landscape of major and minor cities throughout the United States. There is hardly a neighborhood where you cannot find two or three health food suppliers within walking distance of your home. Most products sold in health food stores are nationally manufactured or imported from abroad. Consequently the risk of loss isn't any greater than with ordinary pastries or fruit juices or cheeses, all of them perishables, and not all of them in heavy demand. But the aura of the better products, specially produced for the discriminating client, which was so much in evidence ten years ago when the health food movement gained momentum, is still present. While it was certainly understandable ten years ago when the number of health food enthusiasts was comparatively small, it is out of place today when health food buyers number in the millions. Naturally, like a government with taxes, the health food business people did not feel like reducing their prices now just because they could. Only continued pressure from the buying public will effect a lowering of prices, which are, by and large, totally out of line with demand from any point of view.

The principle of health food consists of the intake only or primarily of foods grown under so-called organic conditions. Organic foods and health foods go hand in hand, although the term *organic* has been applied rather loosely and been much abused. For instance, large chain stores blindly advertise organic food departments when in fact all they have to offer are ordinary foods labeled as organic, because they have been produced from products without additional chemicals involved. Truly organic food is grown without any form of insecticide on soil which does not contain active poisons, such as are contained in certain fertilizers, and processed under strictest sanitary conditions, marketed without additions of any form of artificial flavoring, coloring or additives for the sake of preservation. The same principle applies of course to milk products and even to organic meat, which is occasionally available to some health food stores. In the case of meat, the animal is raised on organic garden food, not given any hormone injections or other so-called health treatments, and after slaughter, processed under sanitary conditions—again without adding any form of chemical preservatives to make it last longer on the shelves or in the freezer.

The term *health food* is self-explanatory. *Organic*, on the other hand, refers to organic and anorganic matter. *Organic* represents the living while *anorganic* represents, in a manner of speaking, seemingly dead or non-living matter, such as stones and chemicals. None of the latter should be involved in the processing of organic foods. There are farms growing only organic products; because they are struggling against competition and are frequently at a disadvantage, catering only to a small clientele, they are in a way entitled to charge more for their product. On the other hand, some of these farms located in various parts of the country also sell directly to the consumer and at prices that are well within their reach. As a matter of fact, prices of products sold at a Long Island organic farm compare favorably with similar prices for similar items charged at a New York City health food store. Quite obviously, the markup occurs at the retail level. Even two health food stores in different neighborhoods will charge differently—sometimes allowing a difference of as much as 25%. These abuses will eventually have to go by the board; but the health food industry has as yet not regulated itself.

The majority of commercial food items contain some element to extend their life span on the shelf. This may be a chemical meant to retard spoilage as in bread, pastry, and juices, or it may be a flavoring agent, as with most jellies, puddings, juices, and other artificially mixed drinks. Not one of the agents meant to retard spoilage is wholesome to the human system. Even in the small quantities contained in food items, they tend to accumulate to do eventual damage to the human body. Their sole purpose is a commercial one, they do not contribute anything to the taste of the product, they do nothing for the consumer, and they are there solely to protect the business interest of the seller. So-called artificial flavoring also contributes nothing to the improvement of the product. It replaces the natural flavor which would have been retained at a higher price and shorter life span.

The modern food industry is geared towards maintaining product salability for as long a period as possible; health food on the other hand is geared towards product freshness and though health food must be stored for a certain period of time, too, of course, removal of certain products when the dates stamped on them have passed is much more rigidly supervised. This holds particularly true with bread and certified or unpasteurized milk available commercially. Bread without antispoilage agents also tends to deteriorate more rapidly and has to be removed from the shelves at a quicker rate. In view of the much larger cost of these items, there doesn't seem to be any injustice in the price charged. Health food enthusiasts have long realized that the freshness of their products is their major selling point. For instance, most fruit juices lose their vitamin potency within a matter of hours after they have been pressed; once bottled, they may last a week. After that, the juices turn.

Purity of manufacture, supervision of the process, and cleanliness of packaging and transportation are all part of the health food image. But there are other elements involved. For instance, health food users will not touch white or heavily refined sugar under any circumstances, preferring the raw sugar still containing most of its vitamin contents. Health food users will not buy processed honey, that is to say, honey that has been cooked and then cooled. They will only use natural honey, which has not been subjected to cooking, since cooking the honey destroys the vitamin content. For the same reason, processed cheeses are not favored by health food enthusiasts, since they are cheeses that have been melted down and reformed, and in the process, of course, deprived of most of their nutritional value by the heat.

As a matter of fact health food and the use of raw foods go hand and hand. Some enthusiasts are determined enough to use only raw foods, to the extent that their system is able to digest them. There are limitations to this of course, since cows have four stomachs and man has only one. The majority of vegetables can indeed be eaten raw, that is to say, uncooked, and still be broken down into their vital components within the body with the help of enzymes. In particular, raw peas, raw corn, raw carrots, and even raw potatoes are a possibility. Those who are less hardy in their tastes might settle for steamed vegetables.

Certainly cooking or boiling of foodstuffs deprives them of all their nutrients. For that reason, diets like the English diet that involve boiling vegetables are likely to be very poor in vitamins and require additives to enable people to maintain adequate health. It stands to reason that bringing a product to boil will kill not only the unwanted bacteria, such as germs and dirt, but also friendly bacteria very much needed to maintain the balance of the body. Moreover, vitamins are extremely effective as cleansing agents in the bloodstream, and thus of vital importance in the fight against disease.

But one need not eat one's vegetables raw if that is not easy on the digestion or the palate. Steaming them lightly without added water is a good way, in fact, the only good way, of preparing cooked vegetables without destroying the nutrients at the same time. It does not make much sense to get fresh fruit and vegetables and then remove the skins (because of chemical sprays one likes to avoid). Most vitamins are found in the peripheral areas of fruit and vegetables, i.e. the skins. I always eat fruit with the skin unless it cannot be digested as with some tough-skinned tropical fruit. Of course, I either obtain fruit grown organically, without chemical sprays, or if I cannot, then I at least clean the skin with hot water. This leaves some residue of chemicals in the skin, just the same, but much less than before the cleaning action.

But the principle of obtaining foods with their vitamin contents intact is not enough. In this day of mechanical processing, many agents are used that may contain poisonous substances, without being directly connected with the food processing itself. For instance, it was recently discovered in Europe that grain grown along highways contained unusually large amounts of lead which would be very damaging to the human system. This lead content was traced to the continual flow of automobiles, because the combustion of gasoline left small amounts of lead behind which were sprayed over the fields as the cars passed by.

Unclean machinery used for food processing can introduce new forms of chemical poisons not present in the biologically clean product at the outset. Even the personal habits of those handling the food must be considered and if necessary, corrected. Just because an establishment advertises itself as organic, there is no guarantee that it observes high standards of processing or handling the foods it offers for sale. The pioneer of American health food watchdogs, the late J. I. Rodale, frequently pointed out the dangers from such marginal considerations. Sending his own investigators to check continually on sloppy or unhealthy standards in food processing, Rodale exposed many food processes when they were found to be below health standards. As the magazine title implies, Rodale's approach to good health was not so much to fight disease with proper foods as to prevent it by continual adherence to a properly balanced diet free from chemicals and other additives.

The Provoker, subtitled *Learn, That You May Live*, is published and written by John H. Tobe in St. Catharines, Ontario, Canada. Somewhat more militant in tone than *Prevention* magazine, this newsletter calls attention to abuses in food processing and recommends certain health foods, as well as warning against the use of drugs. For instance, in April of 1972, Mr. Tobe spoke of "Aspirin, Monster In Disguise Revered, Respected, Welcomed, Almost Worshipped—This Vicious 'Wolf In Sheep's Clothing' May Be The Reason For One Or Many Of Your Complaints." He then lists a booklet dealing with aspirin, available from his press. Just like *Prevention, The Provoker* mixes information on foods with information on medicines and vitamins. There is also a section dealing with organic gardening, since the idea of growing your own vegetables and fruits the organic way is always being advanced by those interested in health foods. Not everyone can follow this method, of course, but there is no gainsaying that food grown in your own backyard is the freshest possible food available. Perhaps those who use their small acreage to grow flowers ought to devote some of that space to vegetables.

In a sense, vegetarianism and health food go hand and hand. It would make little sense to partake only of vegetables if those vegetables were poisoned with chemicals. That which one would avoid by not partaking of meat one would certainly add to one's system by eating improper types of vegetables. Naturally, it isn't always possible to obtain foods grown under organic rules, but the more such food one obtains and uses, the higher will be the health standard obtained, the stronger the ability of the body to fight off small quantities of toxins which get into the body from foods not obtained from organic sources.

We are as yet not at the point where we can avoid all poisons in our foods; just as medicine in the early part of the 19th century had to use the antiseptic method until it learned to be aseptic— fighting poisons first and avoiding poisons later— we must strive towards the day when poisons can be completely excluded from our foods. In the meantime, we should acknowledge that small amounts of poisons will enter our system by way of food and prepare to fight them so that they may not do any harm. The best way to rid oneself of such toxic substances is through periodical periods of purification. In particular the intake of garlic, whether in clove or oil form, is recommended, because garlic is the only substance known in medicine which combines with viruses; it is a strong carminative and purifying agent. The maintenance of proper and frequent elimination is of course the best guarantee against the presence of toxic substances in the body.

It seems ironic that the more primitive way of obtaining food, the organic way, is the way to maintaining good health, while technology has left us with a residue of illnesses caused by its insistence on adding artificial values to natural foods. At considerable expense then, we try to return to the old ways before additives were known to man. A critic of the health food approach to life might rightfully point out that the old days were also subject to plague and other diseases decimating mankind at frequent intervals. This is, of course, quite true; however, the foods are not to be blamed for this, the absence of sanitary conditions in obtaining and handling food were at the base of such diseases.

There is nothing wrong with modern sanitary standards, even those chemically controlled. It is only when the chemical agents enter the body itself through foods that health food users object. A chemical used to cleanse the skin that does not enter the pores or damage the organism in any way is a useful agent. However, when the same chemical agent does penetrate to deeper layers, it becomes a health hazard. The difficulty lies in finding harmless agents to maintain sanitary standards, while at the same time not endangering the person's health.

In this respect, health food users rely heavily on natural agents, generally obtainable in health food stores or from such suppliers as Barth Vitamin Company in Valley Stream, Long Island or other sources. They include lemon-based skin lotions, organic shampoos, soap made from non-irritating substances particularly suitable for children, even harmless detergents to be used in dishwashing. Health food enthusiasts do not rely only on the intake of food as a measure of protection against disease, they are able to obtain various other products produced under similar conditions, eliminating a large portion of the chemical poisons inherent in commercial products used for the same purposes.

A vegetarian should also use health foods whenever that is possible, perhaps even more so than the meat eater. The reason may be that his system, more delicate since it has been deprived of the bombardment of harmful substances inherent in meat, may be more vulnerable to chemical agents than the meat eater's. Although the steady intake of harmful substances found in most commercially produced foodstuffs tends to accumulate and eventually cause illness, it also creates a certain toughness in the system, by which the non-vegetarian's body is able to withstand the onslaught of chemicals somewhat better than his vegetarian cousin's. In the long run, of course, the body of the non-vegetarian will succumb to illness where the vegetarian will not.

Sometimes people wonder how some foodstuffs such as almonds and nuts can be designated as organically grown. How would they differ from ordinary almonds and nuts? Again, the difference lies in the soil treatment, the lack of spraying of trees and bushes, and the cautions observed in harvesting and packaging of the product. When a substance is inherently harmful to the body, whether it is produced under high or low standards, substitutes are suggested by the health foods users. For instance, chocolate is certainly not a useful substance for long-term use. It causes tooth decay, constipation, and in some cases acts as a stimulant at times when stimulation is not wanted. The health food industry has therefore created a similar substance from the fruit of the St. John's Bread tree called carob. Carob, when treated with raw sugar, tastes and looks exactly like good chocolate. Caffein-free coffees are part and parcel of any health food store. Substitutes such as fig coffee or malt coffee are also suggested for those who want to avoid the intake of ordinary coffee.

A vegetarian may drink coffee, tea or cocoa, but a wise vegetarian will restrict the intake of these substances to minimal amounts. He would be better off without them. But there are times when a stimulant is required. Fortunately, there are other stimulants which do not create the same health hazards as *caffein* or *tein*. *Gota Cola* and certain East Asian teas offer stimulation without a kickback. Extracts of ginseng root also are useful in this respect.

In the United States, the burden of supplying organic foods lies with the health food stores, whether individual stores or chains. Lately, some large commercial outfits have actually gone into chains, such as MCA. In Europe, especially in Germany and Austria, health foods are generally carried by a large number of pharmacies, termed *reform pharmacies*. They do not carry fresh vegetables or meats, as some American health food stores do, but they do carry a large selection of cereals, additives, breads, carob products and other products capable of being stored for considerable periods of time without deterioration or need for preservatives.

The trouble with maintaining health food standards is that you have to think of side effects not generally associated with the food products themselves. The water you use to cook vegetables in, or only to steam in, may be polluted and chemicals may enter the foodstuffs by that route; or the water you drink may be strongly flavored with fluoride or other chemical agents, and these poisons may enter your system either directly by drinking it or by washing your foods with it. Ideally speaking, therefore, health foods should only be washed or cooked in chemically free water.

In the United States bottled water derived from safe and natural wells is being used extensively in lieu of drinking water taken from the tap. It is a sad comment upon life in modern times that we can no longer drink the water of our water system with impunity. Not only does ordinary tap water, especially in big cities, have a horrible taste it also contains all sorts of unwanted toxins. Some of the New York

City water, for instance, is derived from the Hudson River, one of the most polluted streams in the world. Despite assurances that pollution elimination plants are in operation and that the water is in fact totally filtered of these harmful agents, the doubt remains as strong as ever. Most vegetarians and health food users have long since switched to bottled water, chiefly derived from mountain sources, such as the Mount Valley wells or some particularly clear wells in the mountainous regions of Arkansas.

Naturally, buying one's table water adds to the budget. But even this is not always a guarantee of obtaining the very best. In an article entitled "A Study Of Bottled Water Finds Some Samples Dirty," *The New York Times* of March 2, 1973, pointed to the fact that "An Environmental Protection Agency investigation of selected segments of the bottled water industry indicates that the water is often dirty. . . . In what was conceded to be a small survey, covering about 5% of the companies in the field, the E.P.A.'s water supply division examined the operations and product of 25 concerns in Connecticut, Ohio, Texas and California. Fifty samples of their output were put through laboratory analysis. Of the fifty samples, according to a pending E.P.A. report, four contained coliform organisms, a standard indicator of the possible presence of disease causing bacteria. Coliforms are usually of human or animal intestinal origin and are often associated with sewage. Another sample contained an excess of lead that could not be traced to the water's origin. In addition, there were instances of discrepancies between the samples' chemical contents and label listings. . . . In many cases, bottling was not performed under sanitary conditions."

Obviously, the bottling industry, shaken by this negative report, is taking measures to police itself more fully. The health food industry is by no means perfect. There are bad examples even among the well-intentioned. But as the health food industry grows it becomes more and more aware of its responsibilities to the public, and it also comes at an increasing rate under the supervision of certain federal inspection agencies. Under those circumstances standards are likely to be sufficiently safe to eliminate the element of risk at least to the point where the intake of health food is nearly always safe. Exceptions due to improper handling or processing may of course occur, but if I had a choice between taking this very small risk or taking the very considerable risk of using ordinary foodstuffs, I would bet on the health food approach.

When Dr. Louis Pasteur discovered the process known as pasteurization, he was justly hailed as one of the pioneers of medicine. In pasteurization, a heat process kills harmful bacteria in the food or liquid subjected to the process. Because 19th century cows suffered greatly from tuberculosis, pasteurizing the milk was a safety device which eliminated the dangers from bovine tuberculosis in humans. From that day onward, all our milk has been pasteurized except, of course, small quantities called *certified milk* available in the United States, or some milk taken by the consumer on the spot, where the quality of the milk is known to the farmer and the cows supervised constantly for possible signs of disease. But nutritionists discovered, as time went on, that in pasteurizing the milk, the process also killed all nutritional values, especially the vitamins in the milk. Thus along with the bad bacteria, the good bacteria so necessary to the body were also being eliminated, and what resulted was an entirely safe and pleasant drink without much nutritional value left.

Consequently, some people prefer so-called certified milk. That is milk which has not been pasteurized but which comes from cows constantly under medical supervision, produced under highest cleanliness standards and tested continuously. Such milk is not homogenized either, meaning that its natural balance of skim milk and cream are maintained precisely as nature provided it. The removal of fatty substances from milk disturbs this balance and so-called skim milk can be harmful to those drinking it because of the calcium content imbalance found in such milk products. When raw milk is taken directly from the farmer one may, of course, boil it and cool it. Although this will also eliminate harmful bacteria, it is not as destructive to vitamins as flash pasteurization by much stronger heat processes. Flash pasteurization, incidentally, is also being widely used nowadays to make apple juice and other fruit juices free of spoilage. Thus such beverages can be stored almost indefinitely. They never lose their flavor and they have nothing else to lose, having already lost their vitamin content at the beginning.

Much is being made of the need to control pests and the alleged danger to fruit and vegetables from insects. However, the only danger to the crop from insects is in the destruction of part of it. Insects do not poison the fruit or vegetable they touch; they merely eat it. If one is willing to accept a certain percentage of loss, due to insects, and eliminates the damaged fruit or vegetables, using only that which is free of insects—which is usually the bulk of the crop—one has not only a clean and safe crop, but a strong natural fertilizer as well. Using the damaged fruit or vegetable as the base for next season's crop, one is in effect recycling part of the crop and thus maintains a stronger bond between soil and that which grows upon it.

Although some health food enthusiasts will not agree with me, I am opposed to any form of fertilizer derived from the excretions of animals since they are bound to contain harmful germs. I am also opposed to most chemical or artificial fertilizers since alien substances are added to the soil by them, much of it on the surface where it can be absorbed into the plant or vegetable. I am, however, in favor of natural fertilizers such as part of last season's crop, which in spoiling will provide the soil with sufficient chemicals to improve the following season's crop without adding anything harmful. In this way one is more closely following the natural rhythm of things, since that is exactly the way it happens in nature. A tree may die and fall to the ground, but eventually it is absorbed by the soil and helps to stimulate other trees' growth around it.

Fortunately, American law requires that all ingredients in a foodstuff be listed on the outside of the package. Thus we are in a position of determining by ourselves what we are about to eat. In other countries this is not the case. If you have bought a foodstuff and are in doubt about its usefulness to your body, you need only study the label; if you find that there are one or more additives of a chemical nature, either termed preservatives, or artificial flavoring, or artificial coloring, don't touch it.

There are, of course, many food products available in ordinary stores which do not contain any additives whatsoever. Additives, one must remember, are put into the food product only when they are actually required. Some foodstuffs do not require additives; for instance, jellies and marmelades contain sufficient sugar in themselves to be able to hold out for long periods of time on the shelves. But of course they do contain white sugar, which is also harmful. Pineapple comes packaged in its own juice, which acts as a preserving factor and is not harmful. Long before artificial preservatives were discovered, foodstuffs were preserved by one of two ways: by adding salt or by adding sugar. Neither method is harmful, although the salty method is far from pleasant. Pickling is another way of preserving a foodstuff without causing any harm to the one who eats it. On the other hand, adding too much salt to a butter or certain cheeses, which is done to extend their life spans, is not conducive to good taste, and in the long run harmful to our bodies, since salt is a water retention agent and too much of it can be damaging to the system.

In increasing instances, books dealing with health food subjects and vegetarianism are sold in health food stores as well. World Health Food Stores, where I do most of my shopping, maintains what amounts to a considerable library shelf, so that people purchasing certain foods may learn why they are doing so. I have also found that the salespeople in some such stores are pretty good nutrition counselors. While they do not replace the services of a professional medical nutritionist, they may come in handy to those who are new to the health food world. After all, when it comes to your body, you can never ask enough questions to be sure you do the right thing.

CHAPTER FIVE
VEGETARIAN PRINCIPLES IN MEDICINE

When one is a vegetarian, one approaches ill health and the entire profession of medicine with a totally new look: meat eaters accept a certain degree of bad health and consult medical doctors in varying degrees. Most vegetarians, however, consider ill health an abnormal state which must be prevented rather than fought when it comes into being. Since almost all vegetarians are in various degrees interested in the occult and have knowledge of psychic healing principles, they are probably also aware of the theories underlying unorthodox healing, which teach that perfect health is normal and ill health is abnormal and due to certain imbalances existing in the body and mind.

A vegetarian, whether of the Vegan variety, a Fructarian—that is to say the most extreme form of Veganism—or one of the moderate approaches, such as Lactarian or Ovo-lactarian, follows the path of vegetarianism because he considers it a better way to preserve one's health. Even if the call to become a vegetarian is based entirely upon moral principles, such vegetarians are fully aware of the health implications as well. Secondary food sources breed ill health; primary food sources help build strength and good health. These cardinal principles are known to every vegetarian and as a result of it, a vegetarian will less likely accept the incidence of illness than an ordinary meat eater would. A vegetarian assumes that illness is due to one of two factors: his lack of adherence to the proper diet, knowingly or unknowingly, or negative thought processes. Even vegetarians have accidents, of course, and they cannot easily be blamed on wrongful thinking, except perhaps in an indirect way.

Vegetarians approach their state of ill health entirely differently from other people. To begin with, they will not accept it as easily as others might, attempting first of all to correct the state of imbalance within themselves through dietary methods. If that fails, vegetarians may of course consult medical doctors. Their choice of such a doctor may also be influenced by their philosophical outlook. For instance, I cannot think of a vegetarian letting a doctor totally hostile to vegetarian principles treat him. Most doctors are hostile to vegetarian ideas, some are not, in fact some are even vegetarians themselves. At the very least a physician should be open-minded on the subject to instill the necessary confidence in his patient which is of vital importance for a speedy recovery from illness.

But not only does the selection of a physician enter the picture, the application of treatment and medicines also may be at variance with meat eaters. For instance, a vegetarian will not want to take synthetic vitamins or synthetic products of any kind if natural ones exist. To the prescribing physician there may not seem to be any difference.

Vegetarians are frequently familiar with the Edgar Cayce Foundation's approach to health. Cayce considered the body a function of the mind, rather than a structure as conventional medical science holds. Consequently, Cayce's method of dealing with sickness differs considerably from conventional medicine.

Not every drugstore is equipped to fill a prescription based on natural ingredients. As a matter of fact, in the city of New York with its many millions of inhabitants, there are exactly two drugstores fully equipped to handle such substances, Goodman's Pharmacy on Second Avenue and the famous old Kiehl Drugstore near Thirteenth Street. In Europe, most so-called reform pharmacies can supply natural ingredients for prescriptions based upon other than the conventional approach to medicine.

Treating a vegetarian patient may put a physician into a quandary. If his patient cannot be given certain dietary treatments calling for the use of meat or meat substances, the physician will have to find alternate ways of providing the sick patient with the substances he feels the patient needs. Fortunately, there are no substances contained in meat, fish, and eggs that cannot also be found in purely vegetable sources. It is merely a matter of balancing the diet and, of course, knowing the sources. A physician or specialist treating a vegetarian patient should be aware of the fact that his patient's metabolism may act differently from that of other people, that the patient may be more sensitive to alien and toxic substances contained in certain foods, and that because of his vegetarian diet, the patient may not have taken in certain chemical additives present in meat foodstuffs which might be the cause of his illness; consequently, the cause of illness in vegetarian patients should be sought elsewhere.

Vegetarians know that nutritional treatment can actually defeat illnesses, even such severe diseases as cancer. Treatment emphasizing freshly pressed vegetable juices, especially the juice of carrots and cabbage has been found to be extremely effective in reducing tumors. Large quantities of fresh orange juice, which is rich not only in Vitamin C but also in so-called *bioflavenoids*, has been found effective in the treatment of rheumatic conditions at times, and freshly pressed grapefruit juice is an effective means of reducing the fat layers of the body and, of course, a welcome way of reducing.

What I am saying is that specific vegetarian diets can deal with certain illnesses as effectively and sometimes more effectively than drugs, injections and other medical means. This is particularly important where medical treatment of the conventional variety does not yield results, such as with most cancers, and certain deficiencies. Some people, especially expectant mothers, have difficulties in assimilating iron which they need into the system. Iron taken orally or injected intravenously may not "take" and may be carried off as waste. In such cases a diet rich in iron may work, because it combines the iron with other chemical substances that allow the body to assimilate it.

As a matter of fact, we know very little as yet about the body chemistry and the strange way in which certain combinations work while the same ingredients, when taken separately, do not yield the same results. Many of the prescriptions given by the famous seer Edgar Cayce in trance pointed out how much importance should be attached to a combination of certain chemicals, whether taken in the form of natural foods or already present in the system of the patient, because the combination of chemicals under certain conditions has great bearing upon the result. What Cayce was trying to say was that a substance may act one way when looked at objectively and outside the body of the patient, while it may yield different results, beyond what may have been expected of it, once it enters the body of the patient and combines with certain other substances in a certain way. Once we understand body chemistry fully, a majority of diseases now beyond medical help may very well yield to our knowledge.

Many progressive medical doctors are aware of these puzzles. Dr. Maximilian LeWitter, the eminent dietician, frankly admits that he does not know why the intake of pumpkin seeds affects the prostate gland in men, but that it is a fact that continuous taking of small quantities of pumpkin seeds will prevent prostatitis. Pumpkin seeds are rich in phosphates and it may be that this chemical is involved in the miraculous potency of the seed. Honey, which is produced by bees in much the same way as milk is produced by cows, is an effective disinfectant, both externally when put on a open wound and internally as a purifier. No one knows why and how honey is able to do this. Edgar Cayce has written that anyone who takes at least a dozen almonds a day will never contract cancer. The acid of almonds is an effective counteragent against the formation of *wild* cells, it appears, and Cayce has made a point of advising his followers that cancer is much easier to prevent than to cure once it has occurred in the body. Papaya juice is highly recommended as an alkalizer. The fruit itself, when eaten at its ripest, contains the important enzyme *papain*. Enzymes which are present in the stomach and bloodstream are the building blocks of the body, mysterious substances which are necessary to assimilate the essential ingredients of the foodstuffs taken in and necessary in various parts of the body. In nature, enzymes are found in fruit and growing things, and not in the meat of slaughtered animals or within artificially concocted substances. Consequently, enzymes will be absent in medicines synthetically created while a chemically identical medicine, when based upon natural ingredients, will have the enzymes still contained in it.

It is amazing how otherwise well-educated medical doctors are vague about the significance of this difference. In a column running in the New York *Daily News*, dated January 26, 1973, Dr. Jean Mayer gives the following answer to a question concerning the term organic foods. "Unfortunately I can't define organic foods for you, and neither can anyone else exactly. Consumers mistakenly believe that all organic foods are produced without pesticides and artificial fertilizers and that they are free of preservatives, hormones, and antibiotics but there are no legal standards or regulations. Therefore, growers or processors or retailers may apply the "organic" rubber stamp whenever they please."

This, of course, is a blatant lie. The only ones abusing the organic label are large companies who want to get in on the gravy train, the path so valiantly prepared by many small companies whose honest organic food had opened the door to its acceptance. There may be packagers of organic food who are less than perfect, as with any other field of human endeavor, but by and large no one applies the label of organic food without producing the particular item under organic conditions. For a doctor to say that no one knows what organic food means, either shows ignorance or deliberate attempt at distortion. A good way to acquaint oneself with the situation and the dangers of tainted food and inferior vitamins available, might be the Rodale Press *Guide to Organic Living*. This magazine, which costs one dollar, may be obtained from Rodale Press, Emmaus, Pennsylvania 18049.

But the term organic does not only apply to food and drink alone, it applies equally to vitamins. The use of vitamins and other food additives is a necessity in an environment which does not permit fresh vegetables and fruits to reach the consumer within a twenty-four hour period or less. Those of my readers who are fortunate enough to live in the country and have their own farms or access to organic food need not, of course, worry about vitamins or other additives. But the majority of people, especially those living in cities, get their fresh food supplies much too late to take advantage of the freshness that was originally in it. Under the circumstances, the missing vitamins have to be replaced.

This should not be done on a haphazard basis. Not everyone needs the same vitamins at the same time or in the same amounts. Despite the advertisements found in the general press, despite posters in drugstores, vitamins are an individual matter and should be prescribed by a dietician just as a doctor prescribes for an ailing patient. A general practitioner may or may not be qualified to do so. Under no circumstances should one evaluate one's own dietary needs and prescribe for oneself. To paraphrase a well known expression about a lawyer representing himself as having a fool for a client, a vegetarian prescribing for himself may have a sick vegetarian on his hands as a result.

Many physicians do not understand the difference between organic vitamins and ordinary vitamins sold in drugstores. Both, of course, are sold without prescription. When I urge that a dietician prescribe, I am referring to the amounts and specifics, that is to say which vitamins, what amounts, and what frequency should be observed by the individual patient. To understand this very important difference, one need only to look at vitamin C, a vitamin commonly associated with general vitality. The absence of vitamin C causes scurvy, one of the common diseases among sailors in the old days, when fresh vegetables were absent from the diet aboard ships. Vitamin C has also been used to combat colds and other respiratory diseases. In particular, Nobel Prize winner Dr. Linus Pauling advocates large amounts of vitamin C as an effective remedy against the common cold, going to as much as 50,000 units per day. Other dieticians have quarreled with this opinion and pointed out that the body is unable to assimilate more than a certain amount of vitamin C. But it is a fact that European dieticians prescribe not less than 500 units of vitamin C at any one time to their patients, and amounts up to 5,000 units are freely available in tablet form in Europe. Vitamin C can be created synthetically since it is represented by ascorbic acid but vegetarians would do well to demand only organic or natural vitamins, for vitamin C can also be derived from such plants as rose hips, acerola and citrus fruit. When vitamin C is derived from these natural sources, it is accompanied by a certain amount of bioflavenoids, whether intentionally or not. Bioflavenoids seem to have a very important role to play when it comes to fighting colds; synthetically produced vitamin C will not do the job.

Almost any vitamin can be produced synthetically, of course. Reputable suppliers of vitamins, such as Schiff, Thompson, or Barth do not handle such products however. Some vitamins can be derived from a variety of sources. For instance, most vegetarians will object to vitamins derived from animal sources. Vitamins A and D are available two ways: derived from cod liver oil and other fish sources, or derived from lemon grass. The effect is exactly the same in both cases.

On a transcontinental airplane journey I found myself seated next to a man who engaged me in conversation. He was surprised that I was being served vegetarian food and wondered about it. After I had explained my point of view, I started to take the vitamins I am in the habit of taking with every meal. I explained casually that they were organic vitamins. To this he smiled, saying that I shouldn't fool myself into believing that they were all that organic. He explained that so-called organic vitamins were a combination of both synthetic ingredients and some organic components, and that the bulk of the vitamins was actually made up of synthetic materials. When I challenged this view, he explained he was the president of a large pharmaceutical firm on the West Coast. Realizing that I could not very well convince him under those circumstances, I finished my meal and changed the subject.

I just love the way some medical doctors and their friends in the pharmaceutical industry would like to talk the health food world out of existence. Dr. Theodore R. Van Dellen, who conducts a syndicated column called "Family Doctor," says, "Many people prefer natural to chemical vitamins or shall we say they prefer them so labeled. Mr. Adolph Kamil, in charge of consumer information quality control for the pharmacies of Consumers Cooperative, Berkeley, California, decided to visit two manufacturers of natural vitamins. He reported his findings in the *Journal of Nutritional Education*." According to this report, the two manufacturers visited were adding ordinary ascorbic acid to the rose hips vitamin C content of their tablets in order to make the tablets smaller. Also, the observer allegedly found that synthetic chemicals were being added to yeast and other natural bases to form vitamin B combinations and that Vitamin E products derived from natural sources were in fact being extracted with the help of chemical solvents.

Dr. Van Dellen then goes on to say that, "In the same journal appeared testimony presented at a New York hearing on 'health', 'organic', and 'natural foods.' The participants agreed that no single food should be called *organic* because all foods are organic. In addition, there is no such thing as "health food" because all edibles in a balanced diet promote health. The term *natural* should be prohibited, because all foods are natural or manufactured from natural foods. The group also settled, once and for all, that there was no difference in the nutritional value of organically grown foods and those grown with the aid of chemical fertilizers and pesticides."

Needless to say, these statements contain nothing but falsehoods and are the expression of a concerned establishment, against whom the natural food industry must have made considerable inroads. As for the *Journal of Nutritional Education*, it represents the point of view of the food industry, as my readers have undoubtedly realized by now.

Vegetarians are likely to turn to organic remedies for illness rather than to the man-made variety. But even beyond the organic label, the vegetarian will look to esoteric forms of healing agents whenever he has the opportunity to do so. Not all vegetarians are well read in this field: The herb remedies of the Welsh physician Dr. E. Bach, author of *The Twelve Healers* and J. Lucas' *Folk Medicine* are, however, gaining wider acceptance every day. The vegetarian's attitude towards what he eats evaluates not only nutrition, but healing properties as well. For instance, garlic is an excellent seasoning agent, and an equally excellent purifier and remedy against colds. Lemon juice, while supplying seasoning to a salad, also supplies a bowel movement when necessary, and parsley not only decorates any dish rather nicely, but destroys mouth odors as well. The intake of celery is said to counter incidences of arthritis. Honey is both a purifier and a sweetening agent, and the pectin in apples and other fruits counteracts poisoning in the system.

There is almost no food which doesn't have a healing property in addition to its nutritional value, provided it is a natural food, grown without any chemical fertilizers and not treated in any way. There are, of course, any number of plants found in nature which are not of nutritional value but which have therapeutic properties, such as gold seal and myrrh, both potent purification agents and astringents. Vegetarians in general tend to look to natural remedies as contained in existing plants whenever they are aware of them, rather than to synthetically produced condensed patent medicines which their doctors may prescribe for them simply because they do not know enough about natural herb medicines. Being a vegetarian certainly helps to be aware of what exists in nature, and there is almost no disease, in fact no disease at all, that does not yield to some existing herb or plant. The difficult thing to know is what fits which disease, and if we spent only a fraction of the time and effort spent on modern medicine on the understanding of nature and her therapeutic aspects, we would all be a lot healthier for it, vegetarians and meat eaters alike.

Many vegetarians follow the homeopathic approach to medicine. Homeopathy is a form of medical healing in which counteragents of natural origin are introduced into the body in order to cause certain toxins to disappear. The principle behind this form of medicine is that the body must be encouraged to do all the healing. What substances are taken are merely stimulating the natural responses in the body to react to the toxins present.

Homeopathic medicine is an acknowledged form of medical science. In Central Europe, especially, homeopathic physicians are numerous and take their place alongside conventional doctors. There are many homeopathic pharmacies, catering to the specific needs of people following this form of healing. What makes homeopathic medicine appealing to the vegetarian is its reliance on natural ingredients for all remedies.

Even more akin to vegetarian thinking is the naturopathic form of medicine. Naturopaths are medical doctors who prescribe only natural remedies and never fall back on synthetic products at all. Whereas homeopathic physicians may introduce some new substance (albeit of natural origin) into the body to cause certain chemical chain reactions which in turn will lead to purification, the naturopathic physician will only rely on direct remedies, and above all on self-healing.

Many vegetarians will carry their attitudes to the dentist as well. They object to the use of injections, such as the injection of procaine products or of so-called laughing gas, which is nowadays used very sparingly because of its inherent dangers. In some people Novocaine, the most common form of procaine used, may also cause toxic reactions or prolonged discomfort. Vegetarians are more likely to accept self-hypnosis or hypnosis by the dentist in order to avoid the need for Novacaine injections.

It should also be noted that vegetarians, being more sensitive to the toxins contained in most ordinary foods, will react quicker and more strongly to the presence of alcohol in their systems. In other words, a vegetarian is a cheap drunk; he may get "high" on half a glass of wine. The majority of vegetarians will not take any alcohol, although middle-of-the-roaders such as Lactarians or Ovolactarians do take wine with their meals in moderate quantities. Although hard liquor is generally refused by all vegetarians, occasionally a small quantity of cognac or brandy is permitted, especially in cases of illness to stimulate the heart and circulation.

Just as those who accept psychic healing as their credo, so do vegetarians accept the proper balance of body, mind, and spirit, and the proper balance within their bodies as the norm of good health. Whenever that balance is disturbed, sickness results. In order to restore good health, therefore, certain intakes must be increased while others may have to be decreased in order to restore the balanced state. Vegetarians believe that the intake of spinach, for instance, in larger quantities than usual, will add iron to a bloodstream lacking in it; that the intake of fresh papaya fruit will counteract excessive stomach acidity; and that the eating of bananas or pumpkin seeds will restore the phosphorus balance in the body, when it has been depleted due to an infectious disease. Thus it is possible in some cases for the vegetarian to readjust his own balance without relying on remedial herbs or natural medicines but by simply changing his diet for a short period of time, until the normal state of health is reached again and the former diet reinstated.

There are, of course, myths concerning the properties of certain foods. For instance, carrots do not increase eyesight. I have often remarked in jest, "If the eating of carrots were truly beneficial to eyesight, how come there are so many dead rabbits on our highways?" The truth of the matter is that carrots contain vitamin A in considerable quantities. It is vitamin A or carotene which is believed to be beneficial in strengthening eyesight. But the amount found in ordinary carrots is by no means sufficient to affect one's eyesight significantly. Carrots are wholesome on many grounds, and vitamin A has many other properties besides the alleged miracle cure for bad eyes.

A chapter unto itself is the use of mushrooms, that is the wild variety. But only the most experienced and knowledgeable person ought to try and eat mushrooms collected by himself. In most countries the art of picking mushrooms is left to farmers and people very familiar with the woods. This is very necessary, since the majority of mushrooms found in nature are poisonous or harmful. The few edible mushrooms are suspiciously similar to others of the deadly variety and only the expert can truly tell them apart. But if mushrooms are obtained from proper sources it is, of course, safe to eat them. They contain minerals in large quantities, although they are of very little caloric value. Mushrooms, however, having grown rapidly in the forest, are beneficial to a toning up of the system, because they draw much vital mineral content from the earth and together with the drinking of so-called hard water rich in natural minerals, may supply the bulk of needed minerals. One should never forget that vitamins are only one-half of the story; the body needs minerals as much as it needs natural vitamins. Vegetarians would prefer to obtain their minerals from natural sources rather than those concocted in the laboratory of a pharmaceutical firm.

Lastly, no true vegetarian will agree to the transplant of organs in surgery. Vegetarians are fully aware of the implications such alien substitutions will have in their systems. The art of transplanting is of course too new to generalize here; but the very principle of it seems contrary to nature's purposes. That which is transplanted is merely the outer shell of the organ not its vital function or etheric counterpart. Consequently, toxic reactions must result in the host's body leading to an inevitably tragic conclusion.

The use of animal organs or animal-derived tissue for surgery is equally repulsive to the true vegetarian. This is not only on moral grounds, but be-

cause the vegetarian holds that the body of animal
and man are not exactly alike, that they obey different sets of natural laws and should not be inter-
mixed. Of course, fanaticism is not called for here
either: certainly, the graft of skin from a non-
vegetarian to a vegetarian cannot be objected to,
nor a blood transfusion between vegetarians and
meat eaters. Except for its medical properties and
classes, blood is impersonal, popular myths not-
withstanding. Whether the use of blood transfusions as such is in the best interest of man is another question. Vegetarians may differ on this, but the
blood of the meat eater is not different from the
blood of the vegetarian.

CHAPTER SIX
THE STATE OF BODY AND MIND WHILE EATING

In an earlier chapter I have already pointed out
how Edgar Cayce, the famous "sleeping prophet,"
has shown the importance attached to the combination of certain chemicals in the body. Cayce shows
that certain combinations of foods when eaten together can cause discomfort or illness, while the
same foods eaten separately would do no harm. The
concept behind it is known to almost every esoterically oriented person.

Every food represents a chemical combination.
Some combinations result in a third substance
when they meet. If the meeting takes place inside
the human system, toxic conditions may result. I
have also pointed out that certain religions, such as
the Semitic religions, forbid the simultaneous eating
of meat products and milk products. The reason is
really not a religious one but involves an under-

standing of body chemistry. It is entirely correct
that meat taken at the same time with milk or
cheese may cause gastric disturbances.

Cayce was probably the first to point out within
recent memory how coffee, in itself not a very beneficial substance, would tend to become much more
abrasive to the system when mixed with cold milk
or cream. Cold milk or cream tend to liberate the
aromatic acid in the coffee. However, hot milk
added to the coffee would not do so but, to the contrary, would alleviate the impact of the caffein in
the coffee because of the protein addition involved.
Europeans have for centuries taken their coffee
with hot milk, probably quite unawares of the real
reasons why they do so.

You don't have to be a vegetarian to know that
some foods just do not go together. Long before I
became a vegetarian, at the tender age of six, I
tried to combine chocolate with mayonnaise with
disastrous results. It isn't because our mind tells us
that certain foods don't go together well that we
become sick when eating them; in most cases, it is
simply a chemical reaction which would be the
same outside our bodies.

On the whole, it is unwise to combine milk and
milk products with fruit juices and acids. There is
one exception, however: if grapefruit juice or whole
grapefruits are eaten prior to having a substantial
meal, even if that meal contains cheese or milk
products, the grapefruit juice will counteract the
sedimentation of fatty substances in the body. But
if the juice or fruit are taken simultaneously with
the cheese, stomach upset may result.

There is a very good reason why the menus of

most civilized nations progress from a soup or appetizer dish, usually a salad dish, to the main course consisting of meat or fish and vegetables, followed in turn by a dessert, usually a sweet. Sometimes a cheese dish comes just before the sweet dessert. The entire meal is then topped off by coffee, tea, or milk. Leaving off one part of such a dinner may help the budget or weight control but it will unbalance the chemical aspect of the meal.

It is much wiser to have at least a token intake of each food category normally associated with a full meal. The soup or appetizer opens the stomach, so to speak, by relaxing it. The acidity of the appetizer may stimulate the stomach's own acidity for the job ahead. The main course, whether it is vegetarian or not, requires the most effort on the part of stomach enzymes and acid to digest it. By balancing the main course between proteins, carbohydrates and fats, all enzymes in the system are equally deployed. If the main course was not rich enough in protein to satisfy hunger or bodily needs, the cheese dish immediately following it may provide additional protein values.

The sweet dessert, which may be fruit or baked goods or a jelly dish, supplies sugar also required in the body chemistry. The intake of sugar at the end of the meal helps to assimilate the dishes eaten before. Finally, a stimulant at the end of the meal, such as coffee or tea, counteracts the natural lethargy due to the heavy draw of blood by the stomach from other areas of the body. In other words, a full meal makes you sleepy; coffee or tea at the end of it makes you stay awake and helps regulate the heartbeat under the pull from the food about to be digested in the body.

One of the problems quite common with vegetarians is the problem of low blood sugar at certain times of the day. Because vegetarians lack the heavy protein balance of the meat eater, they are sometimes hard put to supply themselves with adequate proteins. There are, of course, sufficient proteins of equal value around; in fact, the protein derived from soybeans is superior to that found in meat products, but with the use of vegetable proteins comes a degree of craving for sweets. If the craving is satisfied by the intake of sweets or starches, the body will not benefit but will become waterlogged and overweight. Sugar taken into the body turns into starch; starch does not turn into sugar. In order to satisfy the craving for sweets it is best to take invert sugar products, such as honey, or natural fruit containing fruit sugar which is also an invert sugar.

With most people, the period at the end of the afternoon immediately preceding the evening meal represents a low ebb in energy and mood. In recent years biorhythmical tabulations have been found extremely useful in determining a person's particular energy curve on either a daily, weekly, or monthly basis. Everyone does not have access to or interest in the creation of a biorhythmical table for himself, yet undergoes the distressing low energy period towards the end of the afternoon. With some individuals this occurs at other times; there may be two low ebbs within the course of the day, such as immediately following lunch and after dinner. This will depend on whether the person is diurnal or nocturnal.

The majority of individuals, however, seem to "sink" around five P.M. Unfortunately, our society has seen fit to make 5:10 P.M. the cocktail hour or, in more genteel surroundings, the tea time. Actually, a short rest, in prone position, around that time would benefit man most. However, if activities cannot be interrupted and tiredness becomes oppressive, the intake of some light tea with honey, or the eating of an apple or other fruit will be helpful. Eating a bar of chocolate for the condition will not only be useless but result in the opposite condition since chocolate contains white sugar which may turn into energy momentarily, followed by an even greater state of tiredness.

Those who find themselves suddenly deprived of all energies, perhaps even dizzy and light headed, due to overstrain or emotional stress, may find a glass of freshly pressed orange juice to be helpful. The emphasis is on *freshly pressed* in this connection, since orange juice, like all fruit juices, loses its vitality in a matter of one or two hours. Orange juice pressed in the morning and kept in a refrigerator, whether at home or in restaurants, is just as useless, and incidentally, just as bitter as orange juice taken from cans or maintained in frozen condition. Only the freshly squeezed product has value. The reason can be found in the rapid deterioration of vitamins and other vital substances in the juice once it is exposed to the air.

People may complain that a perfectly harmless food item has made them sick at one time while not at another. This, of course, has to do with the body chemistry when a person is ill. In some diseases the chemical reaction is either slowed down or accelerated, or at any rate altered, so that the food taken in will be treated differently than if the person were fully in good health. That is the reason why physicians prescribe certain foods only when a person is ill, whether this be "bland food," meaning easily digestible food, or protein-rich foods if a strengthening of the system is called for.

Orthodox physicians, as well as progressive ones, take into account the state of health of their patients when they prescribe certain diets. The diet can differ greatly depending upon the state of health the patient finds himself in. For instance, a healthy individual can tolerate eggs without difficulty, if they are fresh. The same patient, suffering from liver disease or disturbance, cannot possibly digest and assimilate eggs or egg products because the very apparatus which is charged with the process is unable to function properly.

By the same token, vegetarians realize that there are no hard and fast rules concerning foods. Eating raw vegetables, for instance, will not cause any gastric disturbances if the person is in good health; the same foods taken when a person has a cold, will result in upsets. Also, individual tolerance to hard-to-digest items differs greatly and should be measured against that individual's general sensitivity in other areas, such as sensitivity to colds, sensitivity to disturbances, noise upsets and so forth. On the whole, very sensitive people in areas other than eating will also show a marked sensitivity in their digestive tracts. Robust individuals are more likely to be able to digest rough food, uncooked vegetables and other items such as nuts, requiring more of an effort from enzymes and stomach acids.

The state of the body while eating or drinking is of great importance to what happens to the food or drink taken in. If the body is tense, and vital muscles not relaxed, the food will be processed erratically—in spurts, as it were—and consequently the all-important timing of the process will be interfered with. The same, of course, happens when one eats or drinks too quickly, swallows the wrong way by swallowing some air as well as the food or liquid, or in general interferes with the normal, measured flow of the intake of food or drink into the system.

Although this vegetarian is by no means a perfect example of how a vegetarian should eat, ideally vegetarians do not rush their meals, but allow their bodies to be in a fully relaxed state prior to eating or drinking. This isn't always possible, but a few minutes before mealtime some form of relaxing exercise can do wonders. Here are some don'ts when it comes to eating, whether you are a vegetarian or not.

1. Don't eat or drink after running.

2. Don't eat or drink when overheated or frozen. Permit your body to assume the temperature of the environment, or as much of it as it is able to in a short time.

3. Don't eat or drink immediately following a coughing or sneezing spell. Your muscular apparatus may be in a state of disarrangement and will require several minutes to adjust itself to normal.

4. Don't eat or drink when emotionally disturbed or immediately after you have had a traumatic experience of any kind. The reason for this is that your acid glands are in an abnormal state of activity at such times, secreting far more acid than is necessary for the proper digestion of food and drink. Emotional upsets automatically activate certain glands in the body, especially the acid producing glands in the stomach, and the sweat glands. It is therefore unwise to

burden the glandular system with the job
of digesting food or drink at a time when
they are strained by emotional stimuli
passed along the nerve fibers.

Whether vegetarian or meat eater, one should
take one's food or drink either seated or standing
upright, and not prone. It is true that the ancient
Romans liked to take their meals while stretched
out on couches, but the upper part of the torso,
containing the esophagus, was usually erect, with
one arm supporting the trunk. In the case of ill individuals, bedridden and unable to sit upright, this
is, of course, not possible. But the human system is
so constructed that food should go from top to bot-
tom, allowing for gravity and weight. Changing the
position while eating can cause gastric upsets, air
bubbles in the system and improper digestion. In
the case of the astronauts in space, where weight-
lessness prevails, the intake of food and drink is
nevertheless possible in the conventional manner.
Food and drink are not simply dropped down
through the gullet into the stomach; they are processed in a spastic movement by the peristaltic canal
and this system works whether there is gravity or
not. But even in space, astronauts eat their meals
sitting down or standing up.

There are a number of exercises designed to relax
the bodily mechanism prior to the intake of food or
drink. Deep breathing three or four times in a row,
followed by a sighing type of sound will help start
the body to relax. Bending down slowly and then
raising the trunk again a few times can also be useful. Breathing exercises are particularly useful since
they perform two functions simultaneously: they
relax the muscular apparatus and they expel toxic

substances from the lungs and blood stream. Probably the best of all exercises are various forms of yoga. This applies equally to simple breathing techniques as to the more complicated postures which are held for a certain period of time. In this respect, yoga is the opposite of calisthenics or gymnastics. In the latter, great efforts are made for a number of rapid movements, whereas in yoga the movements are slow, and emphasis is on holding certain positions for a period of time. The underlying philosophy is also quite different: in calisthenics and gymnastics, the body is being thought of exclusively. With yoga, body, mind, and spirit are dealt with as one.

Even more important than the physical state before eating is the mental state of the individual. Mind controls body, mind triggers bodily reactions. To come to the table with one's mind filled with problems, with worries, with unresolved conflicts, is to invite trouble. Vegetarians know very well that an untroubled mind digests a great deal better than a troubled one. This is especially necessary to the non-meat eating segment of the population since the breaking down of some vegetable tissues, especially when eaten raw, requires a greater effort than the digestion of meat or other animal products. We should recall that the cow has four stomachs aligned in succession, through which grass passes until it finally turns into milk. Humans do not have such a handy arrangement. They have one stomach; larger though it may be, all work is done in it. Consequently anything affecting the texture and the stomach lining, such as emotions, must be very carefully controlled if one hopes to get the most out of one's stomach.

The two weakest points with most people in case of emotional upsets are the fine membranes of the

nose and throat and of the stomach. As soon as
something is wrong, these membranes are affected,
contracted, even to the point of spasms. If you are
a vegetarian it helps to understand the body-mind-
spirit combination as well. For instance, if you have
had some upset prior to mealtime, you may use au-
tosuggestion to calm yourself; or you may sit down
quietly in some room where you can be sure not to
be disturbed for a few minutes, and visualize a
blank silver screen in the confines of your mind.
After five or ten minutes of this, calmness will pre-
vail and you may even get some projections from
your unconscious on this imaginary silver screen.
At that point you gently suggest that all be calm,
that every part of your body is relaxed, if you wish,
naming each component part of your boly individ-
ually and telling it to relax. Once you have done
this, take several deep breaths and slowly walk to
the dinner table. Do not allow the conversation to
drift back to that which has disturbed you prior to
mealtime; change the subject, if there is conversation; and stay with pleasant, positive, and stimulating subjects.

How to end a meal is an art to itself. Many
American businessmen still have part of their meal
in their mouth when they jump up and run for the
exit. The very expression, "grabbing a bite of
lunch," makes me squirm. Nothing invites disease
more than this habit pattern. It is bad enough that
large segments of the business community in
America, and abroad as well, prefer to do their
dealings over luncheons or dinner, but the time al-
lotted to these conferences is generally much too
short to do justice to either business or food. In the
publishing industry, in particular, it seems that two

martinis as appetizer are necessary to get conversations going.

Nothing is more likely to upset the digestive process than considerable amounts of alcohol prior to eating. This does not mean that the French aperitif has no value. A small amount of wine can, in fact, stimulate the appetite. The emphasis here is, as with so many things, on the amount. Vegetarians do not take alcoholic beverages to start their meals. They prefer fruit juice, preferably acid ones, since that will help the digestive process. Unfortunately fresh fruit juices are almost non-existent in conventional restaurants. What is being served comes in tin cans, and is not only worthless in terms of vitamins, but presents certain dangers due to overacidity and possible metallic traces.

I do not wish to suggest that one should begin and end one's meal with a prayer or words of thanksgiving, although this is by no means such a far-fetched idea; but I do suggest that one should allow a brief period of adjustment to elapse before one rises from the table. This is not only necessary to permit the last few bites to settle down in the stomach area, but also to permit the bodily system, already working overtime with the initial digestive processes, to adjust to the additional task of supplying motive power for the individual to move around. Whoever said that a brisk walk after a heavy meal was a good idea was not much of a nutritionist or doctor. Exercise after a meal can be useful, provided it doesn't follow immediately upon rising from the table but perhaps fifteen or twenty minutes later and provided it is not strenuous but gentle. A *slow* walk after a good meal is indeed a good idea. It will not strain the heart and arterial system, but it will help the body adjust to the next activity on the person's schedule.

One of the chief differences between eating vegetarian-style and being a meat eater is the bulk of food necessary to satisfy the hunger of the eater. Even if large amounts of protein, such as legumes or soybeans are included in a meal, a vegetarian meal does not satisfy the appetite as much as a meat meal will. This has to do with the cellular structure of meat and vegetables. Vegetables contain much more water than meat. Under the circumstances, a much larger amount of vegetables would have to be consumed in terms of bulk and weight to effect the same sensation as with a smaller amount of meat or meat products. Since the stomach cannot hold this excessive bulk, it is not possible to make up the difference with vegetables. Consequently, vegetarians get hungry again much sooner than meat eaters. In a way, however, that is a blessing in disguise.

Many medical authorities have held that more frequent meals, during which less is consumed, are preferable to three very large meals a day, because they strain the bodily apparatus less than the three large meals. I myself have found five meals a day the best way of adjusting to a meatless schedule. My breakfast consists of fruit juice, cereal, and coffee. Luncheon is either a sandwich or a salad and coffee or tea; around four or five o'clock I have a snack, perhaps nuts or fruit and again some beverage, while dinnertime comes around seven with a variety of cooked vegetables, perhaps some cheese, some sort of dessert and coffee or tea. Then just before bedtime, perhaps around eleven p.m., I partake of a small meal generally consisting of cheese and biscuits or cheese and fruit.

Some medical authorities warn against snacks before bedtime, because such snacks allegedly cause bad dreams, or at any rate cannot be properly digested and lead to overweight. If the snack is small and consists of comparatively easily digested foods, this will not happen. This myth belongs in the same category as the one blaming a cup of coffee for sleepless nights. As a matter of fact, one cup of coffee tends to induce sleepiness, because the caffein widens the arteries and capillaries. A second or third cup, however, would indeed keep the subject from falling asleep.

False beliefs as to which foods are good for you and which are not, are just as damaging to good digestion as are undue haste and pressures. Whether through autohypnosis, suggestion, or hypnosis administered by competent operators, a state of serenity is of the greatest importance where digestive difficulties have been encountered. Vegetarians know that thoughts are real things, and that the proper thoughts while eating can help good digestion. Therefore, vegetarians need not permit indigestion under any circumstances.

CHAPTER SEVEN
PREPARING THE VEGETARIAN MEAL

Outsiders have fantastic ideas concerning the difficulty of preparing a proper vegetarian meal. Either they exaggerate the difficulties of following the rules of vegetarianism, imagining that special tools, dishes, and ingredients are required which must be kept segregated from tools and ingredients used for meat eaters, or they even believe that vegetarian food may not be stored next to meat. Except for actual intermingling of meat and meat products with vegetarian food items, there is no reason why a refrigerator should not store both kinds of food. Possibly with the exception of strongly odorous fish, there is no danger of meat substances affecting the vegetarian items.

Some people imagine that vegetarians want to act the way orthodox Jews are sometimes acting when they follow the laws of their religion to the letter: special dishes, special tools, kept separately from any other dishes and tools are indeed part of some orthodox Hebrew rituals. But the background of these severe conditions lies in a religious belief rather than in any philosophy based upon health or humanitarian ideas. There is, of course, no need to separate the dishes and eating utensils of a vegetarian from the meat-eating members of his family, or to wash them in separate dishwater.

However, good manners and politeness should prevent a meat eater from using his fork or spoon to lift vegetables from a dish, if there is a vegetarian present. Occasionally, I have been served a ham and cheese sandwhich when I ordered a cheese sandwich. The waiter, without the slightest understanding of my position, would simply lift the ham off the cheese and present the same sandwich again. This I would not take. But I would not hesitate to take a piece of cheese from a large plate, even if it were placed next to meat, so long as the meat had not rested on top of the cheese. This may sound like silly trifles to meat eaters, who do not understand the deep feelings behind the vegetarian philosophy. To me, and undoubtedly countless other vegetarians, these rules and concepts are reasonable and representative of good common sense.

There are no special vegetarian cooking tools; however, vegetarians like to use juicers to extract fresh fruit and vegetable juices for their immediate use, rather than buying the juices in bottles or relying on commercial establishments to press them for them. Vegetarians also prefer to have their vegetables steamed rather than cooked. Certainly, the cooking of vegetables together with meat is out of the question, as is the use of any kind of gravy to cover the vegetables. Most vegetarians, except the Vegans, do not object to the use of either butter or margarine, although polyunsaturated oils are of course much healthier for them, quite apart from their vegetarian beliefs.

Many vegetarians object to the use of aluminum dishes and pots because the metal is not a good chemical combination with the foods that are cooked in them. The preferred kitchen ware is made of iron or steel covered with enamel. All forms of plastic are disliked, although not every vegetarian is aware of the essential unsuitability of plastic as a container of food. Pure glass is preferable by far. The reason for this is that some plastic substances keep combining with the foods put into them. Since plastics contain certain poisonous substances, this may not be without unpleasant results. But these are fringe areas and not properly part of the essential vegetarian credo. Nevertheless, the overabundance of various plastic materials, which has mushroomed during the last few years, makes a word of caution very necessary; whenever possible, use glass bottles or containers—especially when infants are involved.

Whether you cook with gas or electric power is

immaterial; whether you have a refrigerator working on electricity or gas is equally unimportant, except that gas-powered refrigerators tend to be more
dangerous, on the whole, than electric ones. The
storage of cereals, especially bread, in refrigerators
presents a problem, since it is a two-edged sword:
on the one hand, preserving bread in the refrigerator makes it last longer; on the other hand, the
moisture contained inside the refrigerator causes
mildew. For that reason, health food stores sell
bread which is stamped with the last day on which
it may be sold, but the bread itself is generally
stored on shelves, not in refrigerators.

In the large cities of America tap water is rarely
used by vegetarians. Anyone who can afford it, uses
bottled water from one of the mountain springs.
But we must not forget that the water in which we
wash our food, or in which we cook it if water is
used, must also come from the same source, or the
entire process of prevention becomes meaningless.
Even the intake of small amounts of ordinary water
can cause illness, and we should never forget that
bacteria, once introduced into the bodily system,
multiply by themselves with the slightest encour-
agement.

Vegetarians use a great many fruit juices. Some
of these may be commercial products bought in su-
permarkets and delicatessen stores. It is very important to read the label and to make sure that the
product is 100% pure juice not a so-called "drink,"
a euphemism frequently used to mean: some fruit
juice mixed in with lots of water and sugar. This is
especially common with certain combination juices
such as grapefruit and pineapple juice, apple and
cranberry juice, and so-called Hawaiian Punch.

Less disturbing, but equally unwholesome, is the addition of sugar to certain juices. I have already pointed out that flash-pasteurized fruit juices maintain their natural state for long periods of time, even though the pasteurization has killed off all vitamin content. It is a moot question which is less desirable—the addition of sugar to natural juices not flash-pasteurized, or flash-pasteurized juices which therefore do not need any additional sugar to keep them sweet. Either way, such preparations are not the ideal choice of the true vegetarian, but are less harmful than mixtures of tap water with syrups or concentrates, labeled as fruit juice concentrates or essences. In effect, most of them are made up of small amounts of fruit juice, large amounts of sugar and cornstarch, and various chemicals.

Another common misconception among outsiders is that there aren't many different dishes to satisfy a vegetarian's heart. The fact of the matter is that there are more varieties of dishes following the vegetarian line of thinking than there are meat dishes. I recall very distinctly one particular vegetarian restaurant in Vienna, with a menu of over 30 separate and different dishes available to those ordering them. At home, one may not have a printed menu to order from, but the variety of vegetarian dishes available is indeed larger than the non-vegetarian housewife might suspect.

For one thing, vegetarians think in terms of unusual vegetables which most people will not consider. It is not enough to include in one's diet carrots, peas, string beans and possibly beets and potatoes, when there are also available delicious Jerusalem artichokes and half a dozen varieties of squash, including gourds, zucchini, zucchetti, and pumpkin. People thinking in terms of green salad identify with either Boston lettuce or Iceberg lettuce. As a matter of fact, there is Bibb lettuce, and three or four other varieties of lettuce which most health food shops carry. In addition, there is field salad at certain times of the year—dandelion which you can find freely in any garden and a number of cresses, notably watercress and mustard. Apples and pears are certainly not the only fruit available, since papayas and mangos and several types of melon can help dress up the menu, apart from their great nutritional value. Walnuts are by no means the most common of all nuts, but merely one of many: filberts, brazil nuts, hazelnuts, cashews, Indian nuts, peanuts, and probably three or four more, are just as easily obtainable if one wants to get them.

There remains the question of eating out, or eating away from home. In the first place, most vegetarians will do quite well in any kind of ordinary restaurant except those designated steak houses. Especially restaurants following the French or Swiss school of cooking will have ample supplies of vegetarian dishes on their ordinary menus. But if a vegetarian desires to be in a strictly vegetarian place, partaking, as it were, of the special surroundings of such places, he need not go hungry either. There are a number of purely vegetarian restaurants and hotels in existence throughout the world.

Those going on a journey might find useful the *Vegetarian Handbook*, issued by the London Vegetarian Society at 53 Marlowes Road, London W. 8. In this guide to vegetarian restaurants and resort hotels throughout the world, up to 1970, hundreds of local restaurants, hotels, and health food stores are listed. London, of course, has many vegetarian restaurants, being truly the capital of the world. New York City is not so endowed, although there are eating counters attached to a number of health food stores and Jewish dairy restaurants carry items generally acceptable to vegetarians. But there is, to my knowledge, no first-class vegetarian restaurant in operation in New York City at the present time. Not so in Los Angeles, where creative people gather. There is, first of all: Help, at 7910 West Third Street, Los Angeles. In their credo, the restaurant manager states,

"Our purpose is to offer as versatile a menu of wholesome food as is possible. Our produce is as organic as we can purchase it, all produce is washed in basic H, a bio-degradable cleanser. Our vegetables are purposely undercooked to retain the nutritional value and delicate enzymes. Most of our dishes are cooked for your health and enjoyment so please prepare yourself for a twenty-minute wait. All our cooking is done in stainless steel, all breads and pastries are baked in our bakery. The breads do not contain sugar, eggs, or milk. The meat and fish substitutes are made from the hearts of wheat, soybeans and other vegetable proteins. Their major job is to welcome those of you who aren't total vegetarians, with dishes that have textures you are familiar with, to aid your interest in a transition to a more advantageous diet. The oils we use are cold pressed sesame, virgin olive, and deep frying done is in corn oil.

"The body should rest lightly around the soul, so we encourage you to eat less and chew more. Our interest is to offer a relaxed atmosphere, where all

people can share one of their most important functions in harmony with each other." Finally, the
manager advises those reading the menu that there
is next door a "Hall of Health" where people can
browse in vegetarian books, or even attend classes
in vegetarian cooking and metaphysics. Manage-
ment adds, "Smoking is not allowed in any building; this is to allow those of you who do not smoke
to dine and shop without being forced to breathe
unsolicited smoke." Anyone entering Help without
an appetite will quickly acquire one once he takes a
look at the menu. There are such sandwiches as the
Vegeburger Sandwich, consisting of nuts, herbs,
wheat hearts, vegetable protein garnished with
sprouts, tomato slice, onion slice, cucumber and hot
German potato salad, and all this for $2.00. My fa-
vorite at Help has always been the Hunza salad,
consisting of cottage cheese, two kinds of sprouts,
sunflower seeds, grated carrots, figs and apricots, all
dried fruits organically grown and naturally sun-
dried. This salad priced at $2.25 is a meal in itself.
Complete dinner including soup, salad, bread and
butter and herb tea comes to $3.65 at this restau-
rant.

The Source, located not far from the Hotel Con-
tinental on Sunset Boulevard in Hollywool is a
commune-run enterprise catering to vegetarians.
The personnel, dressed in white Indian clothing, is
mostly young. While their menu is not as extensive
as that of Help, the food is cooked to order and
served in an atmosphere of candlelit peace. Consequently The Source is always filled with people. At
first only those came who were esoterically inclined,
and some young people who found the prices here
in the line with their budgets. Then the Los
Angeles Times wrote a glowing report on this com-

mune and their restaurant. Immediately following this disclosure, some very strange people showed up for dinner at The Source. Quite obviously out of their element, these good citizens nevertheless sat down to the kind of meal they had never had before.

Somewhat similar in its menu to The Source, but not entirely vegetarian, though using health foods and organic ingredients, is the sophisticated restaurant called The Aware Inn on Sunset Boulevard in Hollywood. The Aware Inn is much more expensive than the other two restaurants named, and far more luxuriously appointed. It caters primarily to a clientele of motion picture people, artists, and professionals. While neither Help nor The Source will serve any intoxicants, you can drink wine, beer, or even hard liquor at the Aware Inn. You can also get a marvelous view of Hollywood from the picture window section upstairs, but may stand on line for hours if you haven't made a reservation.

The people running these restaurants are not merely businessmen trying to cash in on a newly popular fad. They are dedicated to the cause which they serve, and are themselves vegetarians who live by the standards they have set for their business enterprises. In a manner of speaking, they perform a service rather than running a business. Warren Stagg, founder of Help, explains his vegetarian credo:

"We are the sum total of what we eat, drink, breathe and think at all times." Mr. Stagg is not content to conduct a highly successful restaurant business and what he calls a "Hall of Learning" connected with it. He feels so strongly about the virtues of vegetarianism, that he has placed his views concerning it on the back of his menus. This may be in order to sway uncommitted non-vegetarians to come over to the vegetarian side of life, or perhaps to explain to people unfamiliar with the philosophy behind being a vegetarian why people are vegetarians to begin with. Mr. Stagg's "Vegetarian Manifesto," so to speak, states:

"We advocate vegetarianism because when such a diet is adequate to meet the needs of the individual, it is infinitely superior to one which includes the eating of flesh foods. The eating of flesh in any form is not necessary in building and maintaining a healthy body, contrary to the generally accepted standards. This can be proved by anyone honestly desiring to do so. Animal tissue is so highly organized that it purifies readily to the average intestine, which long before middle age is functioning inadequately due to the unwholesome foods, which today form the bulk of the average diet. Fish, especially shellfish, is highly acid. So are eggs, and it is important to know that most eggs today are produced by hens which sit confined in small cages, reducing them to veritable egg-laying machines. Cancer in animals and poultry, bred for food, is a cause of great concern to government agencies. Recently the U.S. Dept. of Meat Inspection stated that at least 75% of all meat inspected had cancerous tumors on them that had to be cut off before the remains could be sold. Few people realize that their juicy beef steaks contain about 14 grains of uric acid per pound and that beef tea analysis resembles closely that of a urinalysis in a lab test."

Mr. Stagg then takes issue with one of the commonest criticisms directed towards vegetarianism—

namely, that vegetarian foods do not contain sufficient proteins while meat dishes do.

"The best of steaks contain approximately 17% or 18% protein, the rest being fat, high in animal cholesterol and water, full of uric acid, and other poisonous elements like coal tar dyes, to make it red and chemical preservatives to retard the decaying process until it reaches your stomach. Sunflower seeds contain 15% protein yet are high in unsaturated fatty acids, sesame seeds, pumpkin seeds and almonds are also high in protein and other valuable elements, when eaten in their natural state. The soybean runs as high as 44% protein in some varieties and the Garbanzo bean rates next."

The author of this manifesto is not content to point out the obvious advantages of vegetarian food served in his restaurant and, of course, elsewhere, but gets into the problem of health issues connected with the meals.

"One can be sure that as long as the alkaline reserve forces of the bloodstream are continuously maintained, the body will have the strongest resistance to any type of infectious disease and does remain in a constant state of fitness for the greatest efficiency and many years of health and happiness. We strongly advise that drinking water with meals is unhealthy. Water, which dilutes the digestive juices and hinders digestion greatly, should be taken between meals, at least four to six glasses daily. However, if one eats freely fruits and vegetables, especially in the raw state, one requires even less water. Particularly beneficial is the drinking of unsweetened fruit juice, diluted one-half with water or a glass of fresh vegetable juice. A certain amount of liquid is necessary in the digestive process, but the water provided in fruits and vegetables answers this need in an effective and wholesome manner. The purpose of water in the body is to act as solvent. When fruit and vegetables form the bulk of the diet and no refined unnatural foods are eaten, usually less water is desired between meals. The minerals in ordinary water have been leached from the earth and are inorganic. The mineral life wave, having as yet no vital body, does not provide assimilable minerals for the highly organized human body. Besides, today, chlorine gas is added to water and, all too often, fluorides, the by-products of aluminum-making are also added, making it totally unacceptable for human consumption. Therefore, we advocate the use of distilled water, spring water, or filtered water.

"The need for quantities of heavy foods, often thought to be necessary in the performance of manual labor, have been proved to be a fallacy. When the right foods are eaten, very little is needed; every teaspoonful of food must go through intricate digestive processes which involve the use of much energy which the body must provide. A clean, properly nourished bloodstream creates a healthy body which is practically tireless."

Finally, Mr. Stagg takes issue with the amount of food consumed in our society.

"Overeating is the second largest killer of mankind. In these days when much of the work is done mentally alone and most people have sedentary positions, it is important to realize the necessity of bodily exercise. A sufficient amount of exercise is needed to encourage the growth of muscular cells, to maintain the circulation of the blood to the normal level and to insure more perfect assimilation of the foods eaten. This assimilation is at its best when muscles are sufficiently exercised and call upon the system for nourishment."

Althought I have never met Mr. Stagg personally, and never discussed my ideas with him and vice versa, it is no surprise to me to have him state in his personal manifesto: "Few realize that when we are emotionally upset and physically tense, certain physiological responses occur in the body. Through the nervous system adrenalin pours into the bloodstream, the pulse quickens, breathing becomes rapid, the blood pressure rises, the blood is directed to the skeletal muscles and glucose is released into the blood."

Although I have deplored the absence of a first-class vegetarian restaurant in the city of New York, Chicago has a very good one in the Green Planet Restaurant, at 2470 North Lincoln Avenue. Here, too, books are available to those wishing to read up on vegetarian philosophy, possibly while they wait for their individual dishes to be made ready. Here as with most vegetarian restaurants, smoking is out, and patrons are advised that only organic foods are being used in the preparation of their meals.

I found particularly enticing the Green Planet statement concerning the condiments found on the tables. "Condiments on the tables consist of: one, Hawaiian honey from the smog free, rain washed Lehua and Kiawae blossoms of Hawaii; two, salt from the sea and thus rich in nature's own minerals; three, soy sauce called Tamari because it is

aged in oak barrels for eighteen months to enhance
its flavor; and four, spike, a vegetable seasoning
consisting of natural herbs and elements."

Anyone doubting that vegetarian dishes can be
delightful, should try their Russian mushrooms,
consisting of "a blend of mushroom caps, peppers
and onions simmered in a delightful sour cream
sauce topped with paprika and served over grains."
Or perhaps the Cook's Salad, consisting of "apples,
celery, avocado and cashews blended with yogurt
and sprinkled with Tamari roasted sunflower
seeds." The Green Planet does serve some meat
and fish dishes as well, but under organic conditions.

Some health food stores also sell meat specially
raised under organic conditions, that is to say, the
animals are not fed any chemically treated food
and are free to run, thus avoiding the storing up of
toxins in their bodies. If the presence of some meats
in health food stores surprises vegetarians, we
should remember that health food views and vegetarianism share many ideas but are not synony-
mous with each other.

Prevention magazine, in a recent unsigned article
entitled "How To Be A Healthy Vegetarian," con-
ceives that "it is possible to maintain health and
vigor on a purely vegetarian diet. But it is not easy.
One should not undertake this kind of diet in a
haphazard manner. It is true that many times people have lived their lives well without meat—Henry
David Thoreau, Benjamin Franklin, Voltaire,
Leonardo da Vinci, Milton, Pope, Gandhi, and Bernard Shaw to cite a few. However, bear in mind
that when these men lived, vegetables, fruits, and
grains still had all the nutrients nature intended

them to have. Today, because of poor farming practices, and the use of chemical fertilizers, our soil has become depleted and every year the nutrition that is delivered to the produce grown on it becomes less and less pure." *Prevention* magazine has a great deal of faith in the value of sprouts. The magazine suggests that anyone can grow their own, in the kitchen or even on the windowsill. "Sprouts can be your lifeline to vital health on the vegetarian diet. While natural grains and seeds contain many nutrients of benefit, when they are sprouted they undergo organic changes that multiply their vitamin, mineral, enzyme and protein content. Dr. Francis Pottenger, Jr. found that sprouted grains and legumes provided enough first quality proteins to be classed as complete. They passed the test which is used to determine the completeness of a food; they sustained life all through the reproductive cycle for several generations, Catharine Elwood reports in *Feel Like A Million*. Sprouts, then, are a superb food for vegetarians and can pinch hit for market vegetables when it is impossible to get the organic ones. Remember to use only untreated seeds for sprouting. Many commercial seeds are treated with fungicides like Mercury, which are deadly."

It is interesting to know that the amino acids, which are necessary to sustain life, are highest in eggs, followed by sesame seeds, soy beans, turnip greens, chick peas, broccoli, sweet potato, sunflower, yeast, peanuts, rice, wheat, and corn. Although the percentages differ with each individual product, the ones here named are all high in amino acid content. But because of the difference in percentages between the various grains, it is recommended that sesame seeds should be used together with soybeans since this combination will combine metabolically into a high grade protein.

Sweet potatoes and corn go very well together also. If a yeast broth is added to a serving of corn and sweet potato, a complete amino acid combination will have been accomplished and a feeling of satisfaction created in your body. According to Dr. Roger J. Williams of the University of Texas, nuts and seeds, considered incomplete proteins, should be eaten with raw green leafy vegetables to provide a complete amino acid pattern that is well utilized by the body. *Prevention* also quotes Gena Larson as suggesting useful combinations such as raw greens in salads plus raw cashews or other nuts; raw green vegetables with mashed avocado dressing; sprouted grains or seeds plus raw green salad.

"The one essential vitamin frequently in short supply in a vegetarian diet is B_{12}," *Prevention* magazine states in its survey of the vegetarian field. "Vitamin B_{12} is associated especially with animal protein. Liver is the richest source. Kidney, muscle meats, milk, eggs, cheese and fish are other sources. Vegetarians who eat eggs and milk in generous amounts are not quite so vulnerable as are Vegans who avoid all animal products and by-products. Remember that pernicious anemia in vegetarians frequently escapes diagnosis. A vegetarian diet is rich in the green vegetables which supply lots of folic acid, which keeps the blood picture normal and masks the evidence so that irreparable nerve damage can occur before the vitamin B_{12} deficiency is discovered. Yeast, wheat germ and soy beans are about the only foods from which a Vegan can get some traces of B_{12}. To be nutritionally safe, it would certainly be wise for everyone on a vegetarian diet and especially Vegans to take daily Vitamin B supplements that are rich in B_{12}."

There are any number of vegetarian cookbooks' in existence, or vegetarian sections in ordinary cookbooks and it is not my intention to add to them. It is probably more difficult to maintain a strictly Vegan diet, but *The Vegan Kitchen*, by Freya Dinshah, published by the Vegan Society, Enfield, Middlesex, England, contains many useful recipes. Among other things, it shows how soy milk can be used in the making of cheese and wherever milk would ordinarily be used.

From many years of experience, I find that a vegetarian meal, using lactarian foods, but no eggs, can be a comparatively easy matter to put together. Ideally, one should know the exact contents of each food item in order to partake only of combinations likely to furnish one with the highest nutrition. This requires either an intricate knowledge of each item or the consultation of charts at all times. If that isn't possible, and I imagine most vegetarians do not carry their charts with them when they go to restaurants, good common sense will take its place.

Breakfast may consist of either fruit or cereals, fruit juice, and some other hot beverage. Personally I prefer coffee or tea, but there are other hot beverages that are equally stimulating, such as Gota Kola, or one of the many Chinese and Korean teas containing stimulants.

At lunch, most Americans are used to cold dishes, such as sandwiches or salads, while their European cousins make lunch a warm meal, frequently the largest meal of the day. Sandwiches can be made up of various cheeses, tomatoes, salads, sprouts, nuts, anything that strikes the fancy and is vegetarian. If warm food is to be eaten, a vegetable plate will do, possibly with a salad as side dish. It is advisable to have some fruit juice before the meal and some hot beverage after, but to avoid drinking during the meal.

At dinnertime, warm vegetables, perhaps four or five potatoes, and a generous helping of various salads would make up the bulk of the meal. This could be followed by a cheese plate, and dessert, whether fruit or egg-free apple pie or some other dish. Most commercial ice creams contain eggs, but health food shops carry a very good ice cream made of honey and goat milk. This ice cream is a little less solid than the commercial variety, but is far more delicious and much higher in nutritional content. As with so many health food items, especially dairy products, they seem to be produced mainly in the Pennsylvania Dutch Country or in California.

CHAPTER EIGHT
THE VEGETARIAN WAY OF LIFE

Philosophies are as varied as man's way of expressing himself. A philosophy is a concept by which a man lives. Some philosophies lead to practical implementation and are therefore the backbone of action. Other philosophies are merely passive expressions of a specific point of view. The term *philosophy* is derived from the Greek word for liking and wisdom. A philosopher is one who strives for wisdom. One can of course translate this also as a man seeking enlightenment, or as a person looking for knowledge and instruction. We should be careful, however, not to confuse knowledge with wisdom, any more than intelligence with talent. But in the sense of the ancient Greek meaning of the term, philosophy is indeed a very basic set of rules and concepts, governing a man's conduct, life, likes and dislikes, actions and expressions.

The average person thinks of vegetarianism as merely a form of diet. Some people following vegetarian concepts undoubtedly see nothing more in it than that. But the majority of *motivated* vegetarians make it a way of life, by no means limited to the food and drink they take inside their bodies. Vegetarian ideas color their every department of life, their approach to other people, their reactions to such human emotions as love and violence, their choice of a profession, their political, historical, artistic, technical interests. In sum, being a vegetarian is being a person with a very definite outlook on life in all its facets. To the majority of vegetarians who view their diet as part of an overriding philosophy, then, the vegetarian way of life is a practical approach to living, which must of necessity result in practical or tangible results. It can not be merely a stated belief, as some metaphysical concepts undoubtedly are, but a pattern of life capable of being observed, demonstrated, and discussed.

Being a vegetarian has many advantages. No matter what work you are in, living by vegetarian food standards is likely to give you more energy, better health, and a more even-tempered approach to the problems facing you. Statistics have shown that areas heavily indulging in meat-eating, such as the greater Chicago area for instance, are also high on the list of crime-ridden and violence-plagued areas. Excessive meat-eating makes man violent and aggressive. This does not mean that vegetarians are docile and peaceful. It does mean, however, that a vegetarian is less likely to allow his aggressive natural instinct to rule him than his meat-eating cousin. Apart from the minor inconveniences of not always finding satisfactory food supplies at work, and being forced to bring one's own luncheon to work, being a vegetarian definitely results in greater clarity of vision, not so much of the physical eye, although that, too, is involved, but of ideas. The absence of toxic substances in the food makes for clearmindedness and for a consciousness of one's own health, far beyond that which average people demonstrate. The vegetarian concept is a clean way of life, and somehow this cleanliness permeates all departments of a vegetarian's work life, whether in terms of actual physical cleanliness, orderliness, or arrangement of ideas.

Even when a vegetarian plays, he has more zest, more of a sense of humor than his frequently dyspeptic colleague. Indigestion, far more common with meat eaters than with vegetarians, has a way of changing a person's mood from positive to negative. Whether this is actively felt indigestion to the point of illness or whether it is merely a vague sense of uneasiness so common when food is poorly digested or partially toxic, the cleanliness of a vegetarian's food supply makes him approach his play with a fresher, happier attitude than most of his meat-eating cousins are capable of. Nothing is 100% either way, of course, but in general, vegetarians make good players, good sportsmen, because they have extra energy and do not tire as quickly as meat eaters do. Their minds are clearer, not having been fed poisonous substances, so they're able to hold their own in games of skill or mental contests.

The society of the 1970's is a sexist society. Undue emphasis is being put on the mechanical aspect of sexual relations, overemphasizing the symbols of sexuality to the point of vulgarity, frequently forgetting the underlying emotional and spiritual concepts. A vegetarian is not likely to view sex as a purely mechanistic exercise. Vegetarians are fully aware of the interplay between body, mind, and spirit, understanding full well that one without the other is meaningless. Because of this, they have a sort of "three dimensional" aproach to sex. They are as keenly interested in it as their meat-eating friends, if not more so, because vegetarians do not accept the boundaries of ordinary society as strictly as do meat eaters, or conventional people in general. There is a certain degree of adventuresomeness in vegetarians, a degree of nonconformity, which may include a freer attitude towards sex.

On a purely physical level, sexual endurance is of course greatly favored because of vegetarian dietary ways. Despite the frequently voiced claim that the absence of meat proteins weakens the physical structure of a vegetarian's body, any vegetarian eating a properly balanced diet, containing adequate vegetable protein, will be more than equal to his meat-eating colleague in matters of sexual endurance. This is so, because much of the vegetarian food is beneficial to the muscular strengthening, to the cleansing and continual rejuvenation of tissues, to the strengthening of nerve fibers through the intake of minerals and vitamins. And since most vegetarians do not touch alcohol at all or only in very limited quantities, and frequently do not smoke, they have none of the problems associated with these two habits so common to meat eaters.

The creative urge in man depends upon a number of factors; first of all, the uniqueness of the personality with which one is born, then the environment and opportunity as one grows up, and finally the perseverance and patience are earmarks of the true vegetarian.

The question of longevity is of great importance to everyone, meat eater and vegetarian alike. Individual cases will always exist that seem to defy any rules or statistical findings. We frequently hear of the tough old man who died at age 101 having had a daily scotch and soda until his very last day, smoking his daily cigar and eating all the meat he wanted. Unquestionably, his body somehow was able to cope with these poisons. But not everyone is as fortunate. Taken on an average basis, vegetarians live longer and with less illness than their meat-eating cousins. On purely chemical grounds alone, vegetarians consume less damaging foodstuffs and by-products than do meat eaters. One need only to exclude all the chemical additives and preservatives found in almost every ordinary item of food, and add on to this long list of detrimental substances the cholesterol from fatty parts of meat, the excessive use of frying fats, the large amounts of bleached white sugar, and the hormones and other substances injected into livestock, to have a horrifying list of undesirable foodstuffs.

Added to what a vegetarian does not eat, in order to have a healthy life, should be the products he does eat in order to prolong it. Among the positive nutrients are, of course, vitamins, organically grown foods, foods generally not touched by conventional meat eaters such as sunflower seeds, sesame seeds, sprouts and papaya. We do not as yet know why man dies, nor why he does not live to a longer age than the present average. As it is, man's age has increased considerably throughout the past centuries. A scant 200 years ago, thirty-five was a good average age. Today, people live into the seventies and eighties, and many even beyond that. Undoubtedly, if a vegetarian diet is followed and a degree of exercise and body conditioning is maintained, man may continue to live far beyond the present life span. As we eliminate more and more poisons from our foods, we may also learn the secret of longevity and the reason why our bodies eventually die. But until we do, following a vegetarian diet is the next best thing.

Human relations in general, and man's position in society are certainly viewed differently when man is recognized as a vegetarian. Immediately he is considered a peaceful person, a person who is not likely to become a threat. It stands to reason, that if a man will not kill an animal to eat, he is even less likely to kill a human being or attack someone in a violent way.

The assumption is entirely correct. A vegetarian who turns violent or criminal is a traitor to his own conviction. The Armed Forces always had difficulties providing vegetarian diets for any soldier who would not eat meat as a matter of conscience. To the best of my knowledge, such soldiers were forced to partake of ordinary meals as best they could. This was explained as a matter of expediency in wartime. How it was excused in peacetime, I do not know. I can well understand that an organization like the military has little use for people who believe in vegetarianism, which implies abhorrence of the taking of all life. Consequently, when it comes down to that, being a vegetarian and being a military man do not go together.

But vegetarians are not fanatics, at least most of them are not or should not be; it doesn't follow that a vegetarian must marry a vegetarian, or that in a predominantly vegetarian house everyone must follow this diet. One of the basic concepts of the vegetarian way of life is to permit anyone to follow their own ways as well, whether they are in agreement with one's own views or not. I have often stated that I will defend the right of any man to be wrong —meaning that one must never be selective in the opposing views presented by others, supporting the right to have only compatible opposing views rather than opposing views totally alien to one's own thinking. The right for anyone to be wrong is universal and only the evolution from what I might consider wrong to what I might consider right, but which the one who does the thinking considers otherwise, can have any meaning in the long run. Coming from pressure or even from well-meaning propaganda, the conversion would be superficial or meaningless.

Off hand, I don't know of any politician who is a vegetarian; undoubtedly some people in public life must be, by the sheer law of averages. But I should think that espousing the cause of vegetarianism would be difficult for a politician running for public office. What would he say to the butchers among his constituents? What to the sausage manufacturers, the farmers, the food wholesalers and retailers? Such a man would, of course, have the vegetarian vote, but as yet I don't believe that vote has been fully organized.

One of the serious by-products of a totally vegetarian society, if there is ever one in the future, would be the question of what would become of the farm animals no longer being used for food, not to speak of wildlife left to live its own life without interference from hunters. As a matter of fact, this dreary image has been held up to me frequently as a counter-argument to vegetarianism.

The answer is fairly simple. As for the livestock no longer being needed for food, the breeding would of course stop as well, allowing the herds to find their own level eventually. By natural selection, their numbers would decrease, and without carefully planned breeding, farm animals would slowly return to their former natural states. We must not forget that all domestic animals have been derived from wild animals through millennia of breeding. By reverting gradually to their natural states, they will once again integrate themselves into nature, finding a place for themselves in the scheme of things, living as safely or as precariously as nature intended them to live.

Neither would man be attacked by angry bands of roving stags, mountain lions, rabbits, or set upon by pheasants suddenly feeling their oats. Wildlife too, would find its own level, partially because wild animals live upon other animals in some instances, partially because nature itself is the great equalizer. Through natural catastrophes, through the accidents of food supplies and weather, wildlife would adapt itself to a *natural state* free from human interference once again, as it existed prior to man's meddling.

In such a world man would also find a more natural place for himself. He would suddenly rediscover his hereditary psychic abilities, his birthright as a sensitive human being and learn, by sheer necessity, more about nature and the food supplies found in nature than he presently knows.

Prophets of doom keep warning us about the dwindling food supply in connection with the so-called "population explosion." To begin with, the threat of over-population exists largely in the minds of statisticians, people who try to reduce everything to numbers, without allowing for imponderables and human values. Recently, some very vociferous advocates of the threats of population explosion in the United States had to admit somewhat ashamed that the estimates had been grossly exaggerated. We are, in fact, currently losing population rather than gaining as they had projected only a scant two years ago, alarming everyone in the process and getting on some very popular television programs, such as the Tonight Show where their gospels were embraced with open arms by the host, whose own knowledge of the subject was hardly up to the limited knowledge of the so-called experts.

If we run out of food, it will be because we are destroying nature, not because there are so many of us. Then, too, the food industry is busy manufacturing artificial food supplies, some of which are useless and some of which are usable. The advocates of the utilization of kelp and other seaweeds, properly processed of course, as an additional food supply, have been largely ignored. Yet there are submarine sources of food which are untapped and definitely usable, as well as practically unlimited in scope.

Nightmares of the 1984 type, where two pills represent a full meal, may never come to pass, but as much as I should hope to see the breeding of animals for food reduced in time, I would like to see crops of usable vegetables planted where there are no crops in existence. Many areas of our globe are suitable for agriculture, but are not being utilized for economic reasons, for political reasons, or because they require too much hard labor in an age where more and more men prefer an easy way of life, leaving the tougher forms of work to "others." If we grow all the vegetables we are capable of growing and if we restore the environment wherever it has been destroyed by over-industrialization, we will never run out of food, no matter how many of us there are.

As for the number of human beings on the planet, nature has a way of eliminating large numbers of them from time to time. This happens through war, disease, biological changes in entire strains of men, by a number of seemingly "natural" reasons. By my way of thinking, this balanced system is supervised by a higher authority than merely biological interaction. Whatever the system, whoever is in charge of it, the system is perfect and does not leave anything to "chance." All we can hope to do is to gain as much knowledge as possible concerning its workings and apply that knowledge to our own lives in our own time.

A vegetarian way of life is therefore an answer to most of the problems besetting us today. It touches on health, it touches on our attitude towards tomorrow, it deals with violence and destruction around us, and it promises us improved accomplishments. It does not hurt anyone, it does not strain our pocketbook, it does not take anything from anyone else, and in no way does it force itself upon others unwilling to accept it.

Some political systems believe in the equality of man, then try their best to level that part of mankind under their control to one common denominator. As a result, that denominator is the lowest possible one. Also, as a result they destroy whatever emerges beyond the norm, cutting off much needed initiative, individuality and discovery. In the world in which the vegetarian way of life is welcome, democracy for all in equal ways is not the key to successful living.

Equal opportunity for all, but unequal results stemming from that opportunity—depending upon individual consciousness, individual personalities and efforts put forth, with an acknowledgement to the environment—are the only factors that matter. If as a result of its application some men are more advanced spiritually, mentally and even physically than others, they are in that state due to their efforts and due to conditions with which they are endowed.

This is not an injustice to those who are not so advanced. Rather it is a burden upon the more advanced beings to be the leaders, the avant-gardists who make it possible for the less advanced to see and find the true path.